Restoring The Ancient Paths

Jew and Gentile – Two Destinies, Inexplicably Linked

"It is not the reception of the piece of literature but the idea that makes the story."
— Dr. Theodor Herzl

Copyright © 2010 by Felix Halpern

Restoring The Ancient Paths
Jew and Gentile – Two Destinies, Inexplicably Linked
by Felix Halpern

Printed in the United States of America
ISBN 9781612154152

All rights reserved solely by the author. The author guarantees all contents are original and do not infringe upon the legal rights of any other person or work. No part of this book may be reproduced in any form without the permission of the author. The views expressed in this book are not -necessarily those of the publisher.

Unless otherwise indicated, Bible quotations are taken from The HOLY BIBLE, NEW INTERNATIONAL VERSION®. NIV®. Copyright © 1973, 1978, 1984 by International Bible Society. Used by permission of Zondervan; The King James Version of the Holy Bible (KJV); and The New King James Version (NKJV). Copyright © 1982 by Thomas Nelson, Inc. Used by permission.

Table of Contents

Dedication..5
Authors Note..6

Introduction..9
Chapter 1: Jerusalem and the Land of Israel................21
Chapter 2: Fire Meets Water.......................................30
Chapter 3: Into the Melting Pot..................................44
Chapter 4: Laws of Zion...56
Chapter 5: Unlocking Israel's Election: 101
Chapter 6: Israel & The Messianic Kingdom..............117
Chapter 7. The Jewish Root Severed.........................136
Chapter 8. Theological Thievery...............................154
Chapter 9. Sabbath and Torah..................................171
Chapter 10. Misconceptions (John the Baptist & Elijah...184
Chapter 11. The Gentiles Find Their Calling...............200
Chapter 12. The One New Man.................................217
Conclusion: No More Falsehood................................230

Study Questions...234

Appendices I – Israel's Independence Foretold...........241
Appendices II - Review of the Covenant....................244
Appendices III -Chairman of the Temple Mount..........253
Appendices IV - Jewish Accomplishments..................254

Endnotes...260
Bibliography...276
Glossary..279
About the Author...281
Films and Books About Rabbi Halpern's Family........... 285

DEDICATION

This book is dedicated first to my beautiful wife Bonnie and ministry partner. She has endured the process of this work, and without her strength, devotion, and stewardship of the family, including the congregation, this work would not be possible. She has continually sacrificed her own pursuits for the sake of others. Wives are truly the unsung heroes of our successes. With deepest love and affection, words cannot express my appreciation for your support of this work. You continue to be a source of inspiration and joy both in life and work.

Finally, I dedicate this work to my Paternal Grandfather, Rabbi Felix Halpern, along with the Uncles, Aunts, and Cousins that were taken by the Nazis. Also, to my Maternal Grandparents, who risked everything to lead the Underground Resistance against the Nazis for the sake of the Jewish people. And finally, to my Grandson, Hudson Felix in the hopes that He walks in the heritage of his Father's and truth of our Messiah at a young age—Felix Halpern

AUTHORS NOTE

In researching anti-Semitism for this book, I have recovered an historical awareness of my own family's past, which has elicited only a muted response in me for so long. This book is my duty to close the gap. Most immediately for myself. But also to honor the liberation movement of the Dutch Underground during Nazi occupied Holland. I cannot fail to honor the many sacrifices of my grandparents who hid Jews in their homes during Nazi-occupied Holland. It required a devotion that called for action even on the part of the children.

My Mother, a 16-year-old at the time, would pass through Nazi checkpoints disguised as a nurse in order to find more Dutch families willing to hide Jews. Imagine the risk posed each day, the dangers that were present to those who helped. In the aftermath of the war, it became plain that few were willing to endanger themselves, let alone risk the lives of their children and entire family for the cause of the Jewish people. Most were unwilling to even speak out in a whisper. Praise God some of those who were hidden in my Grandparents home during the war live today in Israel and enjoying their children and grandchildren.

The many stories with their harrowing details as a young boy have revisited me. Stories of when the Gestapo arrested my Grandfather only for God's miraculous provision of deliverance to follow. Though we are not dealing with the physical liberation of the Jewish people today, but their spiritual liberation, such personal stories have become an unexpected force in this work.

Removed by only one generation from the horror of the Holocaust, I believe that such people as those mentioned are truly rare and are made to be soldiers. Fewer have in them the stuff of heroes! We certainly need more heroes today! Of these heroes, my mother writes in her book, *The War Years:*

> "They had the fortitude, nerves of steel and an inner strength that most people only wish they had. It was almost as if they were militarily trained. In fact, they were militarily trained; only it was not any earthly army that trained them. In this case, God was the commander-in-chief who gave them the strength and courage to carry out and succeed in such life-threatening missions."[1]

In this work, my own ponderings of the Jewish people come into view. Particularly, as it pertains to two peoples; Jews and gentiles, who in history have been providentially linked. While satan has forever conspired to frustrate this providence, the relationship between the Jew and gentile has become an important marker of our prophetic time.

Our goal then, is to survey the broad landscape of God's prophetic plan, regarding Israel and the Church, and its relevance to the Last Days that we are in. A landscape view aids us in this, as every chapter will hopefully prompt one to take a closer look.

With new understanding emerging today, new opportunities for change are on the horizon. One such change could be to correct the historical circumstances in the Christian Church, which for centuries has limited Jewish calling and distinction.

Because, this being a first-gate kind of work, gates being symbolic of streams of new understanding, few areas are characterized as strongly by this notion of gates and streams, as the topics of study in this work.

Restoring the Ancient Paths takes one beyond the status quo and the religious mindset. Through it, one can begin to fortify one's own step into the ancient paths. To summarize, since the Jewish people have had a central role in the birth of Christianity, I pray that the reader will discover an ancient treasure in our study, the people whom God calls His Chosen People—Felix Halpern.

INTRODUCTION

RESTORING THE ANCIENT PATHS, COMES BY WAY OF MY OWN journey back to my heritage, and an understanding of my people (the Jewish people,) and Israel the land to which I will someday return. Throughout this work, over 50 vital questions are answered with study questions following each chapter.

To understand what God is doing at this time, an invitation emerges for one to experience God's restorative streams by returning to the ancient paths of understanding that was once foundational to early New Covenant Faith. We examine not archaeological remains, but ecclesiastical ones; those covered up ancient paths of understanding that characterized the earliest believers in Yeshua and its community. We can then distinguish faith in the future age from our present age, and experience an essential gate of understanding that comes forth.

When exploring Institutional Christianity and Rabbinic Judaism, knowing how they forged their paths away from the Kingdom is paramount, not only to our study here, but the bigger picture of God's model plan for the future age.

Our straightforward aim here is to capture an aerial view of these movements, then explore how it impacted the early Church, and how an abiding relationship between the Jew and

Gentile was affected. We must also uncover the Biblical and prophetic connection that the Jewish people have to the nations, and the Gentiles have to the Jewish foundation of the New Covenant faith.

No doubt, many revivals, and awakenings have occurred throughout Christian Church history. None have been so focused upon reconnecting the Jewish root to the New Covenant faith as today. In unprecedented ways, Jews and Gentile are joining with each other. For the Gentile believer in Messiah, reclamation is underway. Composed of elements of the Christian foundation hidden for almost two millennia, the Hebraic or Jewish root of Christian faith, ancient doors of discovery have opened up. And as many denominations are following suit, a new kind of learning is underway.

However, this is not one from the Jewish order of things forward as it was supposed, but from a New, Testament body journeying back. Mostly she is being retrofitted with Hebraic elements of her earliest founders. In a real sense, it is a homecoming as she returns to the understanding of her true Biblical forefathers (Shelosha Avot) Avraham, Yitschak, Ya'akov.

◆◆◆

While many are discovering these Ancient Paths, the systematic sanitizing of Jewish understanding from the New Testament scriptures is being reversed. Now such ancient components as the Biblical Feasts, the blowing of shofars, the revival of Hebrew praise and worship, the observance of the Saturday Sabbath, the day in which we are commanded to rest on the seventh day are becoming commonplace.

Gentiles who find themselves on this path are as Christian Hebraists, Gentile's seeking to capture the richness of Jewish text from the earliest days of Christianity. Indeed, a Hebraic renaissance is underway. When we note a simple truth that Christianity came out of Judaism, something profound and abiding comes before us on the part of the gentile body of believers today; God is giving a sincere heart for Zion to the nations. Now, this can be defined as a "genuine love for Israel as a covenant land and people, coupled with a sense of duty to assist financially and prayerfully the Jewish calling."

But a heart for Zion pertains not only to the land of Israel, but also to the Jewish calling throughout the Diaspora; it is a heart that is truly bent towards the Jew, whether in Israel, the United States, or the nations. It is critically important then, to understand the scale and purpose of this restorative work.

To this end, we seek to answer the following questions: How and why is this restoration multiplying? How will it unfold for God's prophetic plan for today? Lastly, how will it align the Church for her final mandate, All Israel? Church historian Shurer speaks to the hearts of many in the body today;

> "Innumerable threads with the previous thousand years of Israel's history join Christianity and Judaism. No incident in the gospel story, no word in the preaching of the Messiah, is intelligible apart from its history, and without a clear understanding of that world of thought-

distinction of the Jewish people. [1]

Interestingly, this Hebraic renaissance has not missed the eye of the secular world. Dated back on March 24, 2008, a Time magazine article lists, "10 Ideas That Are Changing the World." It states, "Revolutions are happening all around us, one in which is the re-Judaizing of Jesus."2 The article goes on to explain that "for centuries the disciplines of Christian Hebraic's consisted primarily of Christians cherry-picking Jewish texts." This article highlights the cultural and spiritual discoveries that are taking place today, particularly the new light on the Jewish world of Yeshua (Jesus.)

One final note on this renaissance. To this growing Jewish-centric-body, Messianic Jewish leaders are aiding the cause, and it is at the Gentile's invitation. I underscore at the Gentile's request. If the gentile Church fully embraces this and allows these Messianic Jewish leaders to serve and lead them, particularly in the ancient Feasts, the understanding of Jewish culture, and the purpose of a fuller union, an exciting element of the Kingdom can be ushered in. Perhaps Romans 11:11 can be activated in a way not seen in recent history.

The prophet Ezekiel illustrates a long-standing priestly role for the Jew. When in the future time they confer upon the Gentile, the tribe of their choosing, "You are to allot it as an inheritance for yourselves and for the aliens who have settled among you and who have children. You are to consider them as native-born Israelites; along with you, they are to be allotted an inheritance among the tribes of Israel. In whatever tribe the alien settles, there you are to give him his inheritance, "declares the Sovereign Lord."

(Ezekiel 47:22-23.)

PIECES COMING TOGETHER

As one proceeds in this work, a historical puzzle comes into view that is both providential and strategic. God's Word reveals essential times when the Jew and Gentile came together, and times when the Gentile played an influential role even to the point of determining his or her blessing. One place is Genesis 12:3, "I will bless those who bless you, and whoever curses you I will curse."

If the preceding passage is correct, a relationship can be seen holding a delicate balance between blessing and cursing, and one that is not obsolete or part of a past age either. So, when one examines the important principles represented above, we can label it as the principle of "gentile service." This enlarges into God's plan for Israel, the salvation of the Jewish people, the Messianic call, and the very return of the Jewish people to Israel. And it pertains to individuals, governments, and even denominations.

Consider the Genesis 12:3 principles when it comes to governments, particularly our U.S government. Take U.S. policy on Israel and correlate it to the economic catastrophes and natural disasters that have followed these policies in recent years. We expand on this principle in the chapter, Laws of Zion.

Throughout our study, an important foundation stone is

Israel's Irrevocable Calling. First, in the spiritual realm and then long before Abraham, it is an "election" or "calling" that will never be unseated by the New Testament church as early Church fathers thought. Israel's election means to be chosen, and chosen means to be elected. While many still see Israel as this historical mystery as mentioned, the Christian Church still struggles with Israel's Irrevocable Calling.

It is imperative then to recall that the Jewish people remain forthcoming people unto the Lord. One glorious day in the future, the Jew will stand for God's divine selection, fully, they will represent themselves as a Chosen nation as God created them to be. Let's also recall the fact, that no other people group is called His firstborn son as Israel, "This is what the LORD states: Israel is my firstborn son" (Exodus 4:23NIV.)

◆◆◆

The first goal of this book then is to cast light upon the Zionist struggle. We establish the fact that God's overpowering presence never left the Jewish people, even in her darkest moments. We make this statement even in the context of the Holocaust. Though one has called the loss of 6 million Jews, the emptying of a large moral space from the world, the Jewish people, along with Israel, are postured for the fulfillment of all that God promised to Abraham and his heirs.

For these reasons, we will review key periods of anti-Semitism, piece together many dark periods of Jewish history, that we can answer the following questions,

[1] What would enable the Jewish people to rise from the furnaces of persecution and become leaders in almost every field of human endeavor?

[2] Why have the Jewish people survived circumstances where other people groups have vanished, leaving no trace of their existence?

[3] What is the purpose of their divine election or called; divine selection, and to be the "CHOSEN PEOPLE."

THE ONE NEW MAN

In our final chapter, we turn our attention to the One New Man, because nothing characterizes this Hebraic renaissance today than the activity around this understanding. Paul brings the One New Man into a more excellent light when he reveals, for the first time, an extraordinary model for Jew and gentile unity.

Only separated by two thousand years or so, a kairos moment is before us. In Ephesians, he communicates God's intention regarding the relationship between the Jew and gentile, and what the Church was to establish for the entire world to see.

Two passages from Ephesians are essential, "This mystery is that through the gospel the Gentiles are heirs together with Israel, members together of one body, and sharers together in the promise in Christ Jesus" (Ephesians 3:6.) And the following, "Now, through the church, the manifold wisdom of God should be made known to the rulers and authorities in the heavenly realms" (Ephesians 3:10 NIV.)

The above reference to "rulers and authorities in the heavenly realms" takes us deep into God's ways, which we give understanding too in our final chapter. We discover what Paul understood, and how the One New Man pierces the walls of Institutionalism and Denominationalism. When we go deeper, we find ourselves beyond Paul's life, as far back as the miraculous account of God's dealing with Abraham in Genesis 17. There we discover the first prototype of the One New Man, as well as some of the best touchstones to understanding the establishment of the Jewish people.

Continually, we turn our attention back upon the Institutional Church. But within Judaism, particular historical events also occurred that are worthy of mention. Many times, throughout Jewish history, Judaism faced threatening situations over their very existence.

ROMAN SIEGE OF JERUSALEM

The Romans siege of Jerusalem in 70 AD was catastrophic history-altering; one million Jews died, 97,000 Jews were captured, thousands more became slaves throughout the cities of the Roman Empire, and thousands perished from starvation. Rome was so relieved that the Jewish problem was solved that Emperor Vespasian minted commemorative coins that said, Judea Capta.

Rabbi Yochanan ben Zakkai, the spiritual leader of the Jewish people at the time, knew specific resistance was futile.

Legend has it that Zakkai's followers carried him out of the city in a coffin and then led him to the Roman commander, who, in turn, permitted him to leave Jerusalem secretly. Taking a hand full of sages, Rabbi Zakkai began a new school of learning in a small town called Yavneh, which was an ancient city located near Jaffa, east of Jerusalem between Ashdod and Ashkelon. Soon Yavneh became a new spiritual center. A new pseudo-Jerusalem developed if you will, where matters of law were reorganized. And from Yavneh, new legal and spiritual rulings were disseminated throughout the Diaspora; dispersed Jews began to turn to Yavneh for guidance and leadership.

◆◆◆

Surely, with the Temple destroyed, Rabbi Zakkai needed a system that would rescue Judaism from the brink of extinction. Formulating a system based upon good deeds and the study of the Torah, served his purposes well. His followers were then taught that these elements were more pleasing to God. Perhaps Hosea's words inspired him, "I desire mercy and not sacrifice, and the knowledge of God rather than burnt offerings. Instead of oxen, we will offer the prayer of our lips."

Zakkai's new direction altered the face of Judaism by placing it upon a path away from any concept of a blood sacrifice. It then became an exclusively gentile Christian orientation after the sacrifice of Yeshua upon His first advent.

Secondly, Zakkai set the Jewish people on a course away from intimate communion with their God, which the prophets, prophetesses, judges, priests, and such deliverers as Moses and

Joshua, modeled for them. An outward form of ritual, the study of the Torah, and good works came to define Judaism. Through Zakkai's innovations, this early movement, and restructuring was the genesis of the rabbinic form of Judaism of today.

INSTITUTIONAL CHRISTIANITY

To consider Institutional Christianity is to find the early Christian Church in her trajectory towards institutionalism. She births anti-Jewish thinking, which erects walls of separation between the Jew and the gentile, and the Jew from the New Covenant Church. One could ask, was it God's intention that the Jew would be outside the walls of New Covenant faith, mainly because it began as a movement that was wholly Jewish?

Indeed, when it comes to the early believing Jews, they were waiting for Israel to be established as a national entity. They envisioned themselves freed from Rome's rule with an accompanying Jewish government led by their Messiah. We discover this historical view in the following words, "So when they met together, they asked him, "Lord, are you at this time going to restore the kingdom to Israel?"(Acts 1:6.)

Still, God never closed the door of salvation to His people as the early Church wrongly concluded and taught throughout the New Testament Age. To this notion, the Apostle Paul states God forbid. New Covenant faith was established to include the Jew from the days of Yeshua, Paul, and all Jews forward. Dr. Daniel Jester has termed this first Jewish community a "bridge community." They were about to demonstrate Judaism in a new spiritual reality.

CONCLUSION

With new revelations in ample supply today, many questions will be asked. What happens when the body finds the differences between Institutional Christianity and the kingdom, or the roots of anti-Semitism within our very institutions or Christian denominations?

Finding the answers to these questions, quickly one learns that the Jewish resistance to the Christian Church has not always been the glorious message of the Gospel as many have thought. Instead, it has been the Church's internal rejection of all things Jewish. Ponder some of these, and it will likely provoke unknown responses within you.

Throughout, I lay bare as a voice of many crying out in the wilderness, the age-old story of God's Chosen People, along with the appointed destiny of the New Testament Church. You see, history repeatedly reveals that there is a significant role that the Church played in the Jewish struggle. But anti-Semitic thinking was fostered early and broke into the Church. Praise God, and He is healing age-old breaches that satan created.

Restoring the Ancient Paths provides a fresh perspective on the future life of the Church, the Messianic Kingdom to come, and the relationship between the Jew and gentile, two destines that are inexplicably linked to each other. One will discover the Jewish connection not only to the land that we call Israel but the heart of Israel, Jerusalem.

With heart-wrenching detail, one will discover the historical persecutions that have repeated itself, again and again, all in an attempt to remove the Jew from the face of the earth. From past wanderings of the Jew, and their miraculous return to their land, and to their journey through the Christian Church, one will see how walls of division rose that is only now beginning to come down.

One will discover kairos [4] moments in this work. These are times when heaven and earth came together for the Jew and gentile. At every step, the reader is given an opportunity to restore ancient paths of understanding and faith in their own life. Each chapter becomes a gate to go further.

CHAPTER ONE

Jerusalem and The Land of Israel

"Jerusalem does not cease being to the Jewish people why it was during King David's time and still is today; the heart of the Jewish people and its joy. It has been designated [by the United Nations Special Commission on Palestine, 1947] the capital of the Jewish state, but it was and will always remain the capital of the Jewish people, the very core of the entire Jewish people."[1]

— David Ben Gurion

A GREAT SCHOLAR AND SAGE OF THE THIRTEENTH CENTURY, Rabbi Moshe Ben Nachman said, "to take possession of the Holy Land and to live in it must be counted among the Biblical commandments incumbent upon Jews to fulfill." An additional Orthodox Jewish saying states, "the one who rules over the Holy Mount rules over Jerusalem; the one who rules over Jerusalem rules over the Holy Land."

The above saying draws one immediately to the Jewish connection to Jerusalem. Always, it will be their place of personal and national destiny. This comes from a people who have forever envisioned that they would return to the site of their ancient worship. Yet, for Bible students and teachers of prophecy, Israel remains the axis of end-time events and a precursor to scores of prophecies that remain dependent upon it.

The birth of Israel in 1948 was the most significant prophetic event in modern history. Take for example the combined passages of Leviticus 26 and Ezekiel 4:3-6, and remarkably it produces a prophetic prediction of Israel's birth 2,484 years before it happened to the day (See Appendix I.) Also, remarkable, the medieval French Jewish scholar Rashi (1040 –1105) calculates Abraham's birth to be 1,948 years following the birth of Adam.

God chose Abraham to be the individual intermediary between God and the covenant and for his seed. Abraham was a descendant of Eber, an Eberite because he migrated from the other side (east) of the Euphrates River. Eber was the great-grandson of Shem and ancestor of Yeshua (Genesis 10:21, Luke 3:35.) Ancestrally speaking then, Eber was the founder of the Hebrew race we call Jews today (Luke 3:35.)

Abraham's grandson, Jacob, became known as Israel, who had twelve sons who became known as the twelve tribes of Israel, or the children of Israel. These comprised the twelve tribes: Reuben, Simeon, Levi, Judah, Issachar, Zebulon, Dan, Naphtali, Gad, Asher, Joseph, and Benjamin, (Genesis 29:32-23:24; 35:16-18.) But it is the oldest member of the Jewish family, Abraham, which became the focal point of Jewish identity, and remains so today. Through Abraham, Jews throughout history would repeatedly recall from whose loins they have descended, and the nations would also receive their connection. We first turn to the Jew: "Look to the rock from which you were cut and to the quarry from which you were hewn; look to Abraham, your father, and to Sarah who gave you birth" (Isaiah 51: 1-2.)

Second to the gentile: "Understand, then, that those who believe are children of Abraham. The Scripture foresaw that God would justify the Gentiles by faith, and announced the gospel in advance to Abraham" (Galatians 3:7-8.) Again, "Your name will be Abraham, for I have made you a father of many nations" (Genesis 17:5-6.)

Today, the people are called Jews because the word Jew is derived from Judah. Judah is one of the twelve tribes that descended from Jacob to become the most prominent of the twelve tribes. Also, Jew became the prevalent name for the entire people, particularly after the kingdom of Judea survived the downfall of the Northern Kingdom in 722 BC; this was the time when the ten tribes were led into captivity.

ISRAEL'S VISIONARY

The land of Israel has always been referred to by many names. The land of the Hebrews (Genesis 40:15,) the Holy land (Zechariah 2:12,) the land of Jehovah (Hosea 9:3,

Psalm 85:1,) the land of Promise (Hebrews 11:9.) Some 3200 years ago, approximately 1200 BCE, the Jews settled the land. This occurred long before the Arab conquest of Jerusalem in 640, or the conquest of the Ottoman Turks in 1516.

Yet, the modern state of Israel exists today due to one man, Theodor Herzl (1860-1904.) Of course, it is attributed to something higher; God's enduring promises of Jewish return to the land. God raises up human agents, and Herzl was one of these.

A son of a wealthy banking family, Herzl chose to become a journalist. Never did he imagine that he would be the key to the prophetic fulfillment of Zion. While on assignment, Herzl was covering the infamous trial of a Jewish French captain accused of passing French military secrets to Germany. Even though the charges later proved to be false, throughout the trial, Herzl witnessed unsettling anti-Jewish rallies and public outcries, and anti-Semitic slurs as, A bas les Juifs (Down with the Jews,) A la mort les Juifs, (Death to the Jews.) These encounters with Jewish hate during this time, borne a realization within him, that anti-Semitism would not be defeated or cured, but only avoided.

Herzl knew that the Jew needed to be protected from such hate, and understood that a Jewish state had to be established. In 1896, Herzl published a book outlining this idea and titled the project, Der Judenstat (The Jewish State.) The next year under his leadership, the First Zionist Congress convened in Basel, Switzerland. However, few were willing to lend support to the idea of a Zionist state in early 1894. He found that most people were what he termed, Oppositionists, and Assimilationists. These were people that were more concerned with the loss of Jewish wealth than the safety of the Jewish people.

As Nazi Germany rose to power, and horrific suffering began on European Jewry, Herzl's earliest fears must have haunted him. On November 29, 1947, a coalition of nations finally agreed that the Jews needed a haven to call their own. The United Nations voted in support of a Jewish homeland. But part of the United Nations agreement were plans to partition the Holy Land into two independent states to bring about the internationalization of Jerusalem. Also, throughout the process, the Arabs were always making their intention known that they would go to war with Israel if she were granted her land.

On May 14, 1948, Israel finally declared her independence. As expected, the allied forces of Syria, Lebanon, Jordan, Egypt, and Iraq, in defiance of the U.N. agreement, attacked Israel the following day. Israel being ill-equipped due to an international arms embargo was eventually aided by Czechoslovakia by selling her arms and supplies, which turned the tide of the war in Israel's favor—Of course, God would have raised up another nation.

A CITY of PEACE
DEFINED by WAR

When reviewing Jewish history, and thinking of Jerusalem, the city of peace, it is a city defined by war. Even the Arab aversion to Israel today compared to 1948, has changed little. Consider a Life magazine article from June 16, 1967, which highlights the historical Arab-Israeli struggle; "For Arabs, Israel is an illegal fiction created out of former Arab lands by an imperialistic West, an alien culture that poses a continual threat to a visionary brotherhood of the Arab nations that surround it."]2]

Since 1948 and the War of Independence, Israel has had three major wars. The war of the Sinai Campaign in 1956 between Israel and Egypt; the Six-Day War in 1967 with Nasser of Egypt, Jordan, and Syria; and the Yom Kippur War in 1973, the time when Egyptian and Syrian forces attacked Israel on two fronts.

She has endured two intifadas and lives under continuous threats of terrorism. She experiences sporadic diplomatic isolation. Her land borders are surrounded by nations that are more or less closed to trade. And living almost as an outcast in the Middle East, does she derive any profit from the enormous wealth generated by regional oil wealth? No! Israel bears the costs of living in a small geographic area that is characterized by arms races and instability.

Today, Israel's land is approximately the size of New Jersey, encompassing only about 11,000 square miles. It is a fraction of its original 60,000 square miles when David and his son Solomon's reigned. Yet, Arab lands even back in 1947 totaled approximately 8,500,000 square miles. Compare this to what was considered then Israel's administered areas of only 28, 500 square -miles. [3]

◆◆◆

Isn't it intriguing that Israel has struggled for a tiny piece of land in contrast to the vastness of Arab nations? So why is a small state both in land and population despised by so many? The answer lies not in the Geopolitical sphere, of course, but within the Spiritual. There are profoundly spiritual and prophetic reasons that Israel has one war after another. Hence, Jewish history is defined by war!

Still, Jerusalem, the ancient Hebrew meaning, "City of Peace," seems to always be under a curse of bloodshed, whether we go back to the time of her ancient altars and sacrifices, or the history of our modern-day, or the sacrifice of Messiah Himself on a cross. It is the constant sacrifices of men that defend Jerusalem as she struggles to be the City of Peace.

THE LOVE of the TEMPLE

No discussion on the Jewish people can be without a conversation on the Temple. Rabbi's hold to the belief that Jews reached great heights of spirituality twice, both times when the Temples were built. Twice they were destroyed, and both times on the very same date, the ninth of Av, and only separated by 656 years. And since the month of Av means Father, Jews believe that the Father in heaven was involved. According to tradition, it has become the "saddest day" in Jewish history.

Whether we speak of the building of the First and Second Temple or the days of the wilderness-tent-of-meeting, Jews have sought communion with God. At the center of such a historical turmoil, there are a people that have survived and become a miraculous testament to God's protection of them. They are the Jews; only the Jews can trace their history and occupation to a homeland that is more than three thousand years old. Unlike any other people then, the Jews are emotionally, spiritually, and Biblically bound to their land. Rabbi Hayim Halevy Donin states, "It is a land possessed by not only right of conquest and settlement but also a fulfillment of history, faith, and law." [4]

END OF CHAPTER STUDY QUESTIONS

1. Who was Theodore Herzl?
2. What is the ancient name of Jerusalem?
3. Describe Institutional Christianity and its effect upon the Jewish people.
4. Can you explain the connection that the Jewish people have to the land of Israel?
5. What is the significance of the Jewish love for the Temple?

    a. What is its prophetic significance?

6. When did Israel become a nation, and what political organization agreed to its formation and what were the conditions?
7. Can you name Israel's three major wars, and explain what happened the day after Israel became a nation?

CHAPTER TWO

Judaism: A Historical Chaos
"Fire Meets Water

"Israel is likened to a man traveling on the road when he encountered a wolf and escaped from it and he went along relating the affair of wolf. He then encountered a lion and escaped from it, and went along relating the affair of the lion. He then encountered a snake, escaped from it, whereupon he forgot the two previous incidents, and went along relating the affair of the snake. So it is with Israel; the present troubles cause them to forget the earlier one." —*Berkoth 13a.* [1]

IN SCRIPTURE, ISRAEL AND ITS ENEMY ARAM (SYRIA) ARE COMPARED TO WATER AND FIRE. A prophecy concerning Damascus states, "Woe to the roar of the many nations who are tumultuous as the roar of the sea" (Yeshayahu – Isaiah 17:12.) However, the Jewish people are compared to fire as it states, "The House of Yaakov be fire" (Ovadiah - Obadiah 1:18.)

When considering this simple analogy, consider the fact that water and fire are apparent opposites in both their nature and in the way that they affect each other. Fire produces light and heat, the water, of course, provides the opposite cooling effect and extinguishes the flame. But when working together, fire improves water by boiling it and allows people to enjoy food as well as many other things. Still, fire and water are never welcome partners.

Demonstrating what God envisioned for the Jewish people, they were to be the fire and light to the world, and the Jew was to spread the light of the One True God and His principles. Yet like water extinguishes fire, the nations have worked hard to smother the Jew. This is seen in centuries of anti-Semitic outrages, where rarely have Jews found a secure home where a public or government has not demonstrated Jewish hate. And seldom have the Jewish people found peace and security when nations have sanctioned and condoned anti-Semitism within their borders.

Consider the Holocaust, Blood Libels, Forced Conversions, Exiles, and Expulsions. These encompass such a broad spectrum of Jewish hate that it brings to light a sinister plot to eliminate the Jewish people from the earth. If we are to receive a heart for the Jewish people truly, we must understand that their physical part (her historical experience) is part of the whole that comprises the Jew.

For this reason, we offer only a minor survey below. When most only think of the Holocaust, here is a brief anthology of Jewish suffering, so the reader is acquainted with the seven specific kinds of anti-Semitic acts against Jews. Combined, one can see the comprehensive and demonic effort to remove, or persecute, God's firstborn throughout history.

I.   EXILES MARCHING THROUGH TIME

Jews were exiled and or unwelcome in most places of the world and few people other than Jews have experienced. Few nations are free from this particular Jewish bloodguilt as well. This historical reality is true when speaking of European countries as England, France, Germany, Portugal, Spain, also Lithuania and Hungary that displaced untold thousands of Jews.

In 1492, 90,000 Jews from Turkey had to leave their homes. During the same period, thousands were baptized by force in Spain, and the ones that refused were forced to leave their homes. 25,000 were exiled from Holland, 20,000 from Morocco, 10,000 from France, and 10,000 from Italy. Hundreds of thousands were displaced, and thousands of Jews died seeking a new home, while under force, thousands converted to Christianity. [2]   One can only imagine what Spanish Jewry thought at the time of the Jewish Psalm 60: "O God, thou hast cast us off, thou hast scattered us, thou hast been displeased; "O turn thyself to us again" (KJV.)

II.   HORROR of the POGROMS

Pogrom is a Russian word that means riot or devastation and applies to violent anti-Jewish attacks. Hundreds of Pogroms on a large scale brought massacres and anti-Jewish riots and took place, especially under the Czarist regime of Russia and Poland. The most severe pogroms took place in 1881 and 1903, but also to as late as 1918 to 1921. These riots would be highly organized in order to bring great devastations to Jewish neighborhoods, including the burning of synagogues and the beating of Jews to the point of death.

Under Muslim rule, thousands of Jews suffered from 750 to 1900 AD. In 1033 in the Moroccan city of Fez, six thousand Jews were massacred. And throughout the country of Morocco, and especially in the city of Marrakesh, a profuse amount of anti-Jewish persecutions and massacres took place.

III. ALWAYS BEING BRANDED

Jews have long been branded by society as different. The medieval depiction of Jews as devils is documented by Joshua Trachtenberg's, The Devil and the Jews (New Haven: Yale University Press 1941.)

There is the modern-day notion of money mongers and old fables describing a people who have horns. But when Jews were forced to wear unique labels to tell them apart from gentiles, it began a practice both notorious and demeaning. In 1215 that is exactly what the Pope decreed at the 4th Lateran Council when he ordered that all Jews wear a yellow badge upon their breast to distinguish them from gentile Christians. In 1317 the Catholic Church at the Ravenna Council declared the following.

> "That they (Jews) ought not to be tolerated to the detriment or severe injury of the faithful, because it frequently happens that they return to Christian's contumely for favors, contempt for familiarity.

33

Therefore, the provincial of Ravenna some time since...thinking that many scandals have arisen from them commingling with Christians, it is decreed that they should wear a wheel of yellow cloth on their outer garment, and their women alike wheel on their heads, so that they may be distinguished from Christians." [3].

◆◆◆

a. Jews were not allowed to hold public office, Synod of Clermont 53.

b. Jews were not allowed to show themselves in the street during Passion Week, Third Synod of Orleans, 538.

c. Burning of the Talmud and other Jewish books, 12th Synod of Toledo, 681.

d. Christians were not permitted to patronize Jewish doctors, Trulanic Synod, 692.

e. Jews were required to pay taxes for the support of the Roman Church to the same extent as Christians, Synod of Gerona, 1078.

f. Christians were not allowed to attend Jewish ceremonies, Synod of Vienna, 1267.

g. Compulsory Jewish ghettos, Synod of Breslau, 1267.

h. Jews were not allowed to obtain academic degrees, Council of Basel, Session XIX. [4]

SPECIAL NOTE: Christian church legislation against Jews was so pervasive that Hitler utilized them to model his own anti-Semitic legislation. For instance, when he re-instituted the Nazi policy of labeling the Jews during the Holocaust, as noted earlier, the Catholic Church first modeled it. But Hitler brought the practice to new heights when he posted reminders throughout Germany that said," When you see this symbol [the yellow star,] know your true enemy, "1941."

IV. CONVERSION of JEWISH CHILDREN

In the context of the historical horrors given above, Judaism views Christianity through a history of great suffering. Unquestionably, such horrific actions could not have come from genuinely transformed believers in Messiah. But they were still done in the name of Christianity.

For example, imagine taking Jewish children at the complete disregard of their parents to convert them. Yet episodes as these of forced conversions took place throughout Europe, Persia, and Morocco, mainly from 460 AD to as late as 1858. In 1145 it took place in the country of Morocco; Jews were even forced to convert to Islam.

The Canonist decree during the nineteenth century by Russian authorities is the most notorious. Jewish children were seized and forced to serve in the Czar's army, then shipped off to distant locations for as much as 25 years. Russian authorities would then force the children to lose all contact with Jews for them to adopt the local religion. Conversions were also forced upon the Jews throughout the Byzantine Empire in the years 640 to 930.

In 1242, the Jews of Spain were forced to attend conversion sermons by order of King James I of Aragon, while massive burnings of the Talmud took place in Paris during this time. An event took place in England in 1222 that genuinely characterizes the social paranoia and hatred against the Jew. It occurred when a young university student was burned alive for marrying a Jew and converting to Judaism.

In light of these events, consider the central prayer of Kol Nidre generally recited during Yom Kippur, it renounces all pledges, that captors and misled Christian zealots forced upon the Jew:

> **Kol Nidre:** All vows, oaths, and promises which we may be forced to take between this Yom Kippur and the next, of these, we repent and these, we renounce. Let them be nullified and voided, and let us be absolved and released. Let personal vows, pledges, be considered neither vows nor pledges nor oaths."

V. BLOOD LIBELS

Historically, a blood libel is a lie or fable that accuses Jews of taking a Christian child's blood for ritual purposes. Specifically, taking the blood to make matzo for Passover. As ridiculous as these charges sound, many believed it even though ingesting

36

blood was strictly prohibited in the Torah (Leviticus 17:10-14.) Blood libel fantasies became a regular charge from Christian anti-Semites during the Middle Ages. So rampant was it, that the Muslim world repeated it by substituting a Muslim child for a Christian child and hamantashen for matzo.

The first recorded blood libel took place in England in 1144 AD. It was a twelve-year-old English boy whose violent death was attributed to the Jewish community of Norwich, merely because he regularly came into contact with Jews. His name was William of Norwich. Later Norwich was venerated as a martyr, though his death was never solved. Nevertheless, the allegation of ritual murder or blood libel was believed to be the cause of his death.

One final note, Hitler renewed the superstition of the blood libel when on May 1, 1934, in the Nazi newspaper Der Sturmer, 5, he devoted the regular weekly edition to this Jewish ritual by posting illustrations of rabbis sucking the blood of German children.

VI. TRIBUNALS and CRUSADES

Of all the actions in Jewish history, one of the most feared and hated words has been the term "Inquisition." It means "inquiry." For gentiles, it also came to symbolize extremism, ruthlessness, and torture. It was during the Thirteenth century that church courts were formed to investigate Christian believers to hunt them down and accuse them of being heretics.

For Jews, these so-called church officials would enter

Synagogues on Saturday with an armed mob behind them. Jews were then interrogated and pressured to convert. Rarely could Jews argue or refuse this forced method of conversion during this time.

But it was the "Crusades," holy wars, which were launched to cleanse the Holy Land of both Jews and Muslims, which left the walls of Jewish history stained with blood. Through these misled zealots, Christian Crusaders went on so-called "missions from God" while inciting entire mobs to massacre whole Jewish communities.

The battle cry of these Crusaders was, "Before attempting to revenge ourselves upon the Muslim unbelievers, let us first avenge ourselves upon the 'killers of Christ living in our midst!" Appallingly, the appeal to joining the Crusades was that one could have all debts canceled. During this dark time, thousands of Jews were slaughtered for the cause of Christian missions. It was said, "so great was the killing and the torturing, so great was the Jews bravery in accepting pain and death without denying their God, that an entire generation died al Kiddush Ha-Shem, for the sanctification of God's name."[6]

The launching of the First Crusade ended ten centuries of comparative peace for the Jewish people and ushered in a period of persecution that had rarely occurred. The first of these Crusades took place in the year 1096, with more Crusades following in the years 1146, 1187, and 1202. The Crusades became internationalized in AD 1078 when Pope

Gregory VII forbade any Christian kingdom from hiring Jews.

The principle demand upon the Jews was to accept baptism, though in most cases, Christian conversion only allowed one to die a quicker death. Ironically, the Jews fared much better under Saladin, the Sultan of Egypt after he defeated the Crusaders, this may be due to Saladin's court physician who was the great Jewish scholar, Maimonides.

VII. ANNIHILATION CAMPAIGNS

Wanting to annihilate the Jewish people is something that goes back not thousands of years, but only as recent as 350 years to date. And though no persecution in Jewish history is greater and more infamous than the Holocaust, one of two central campaigns launched against the Jew, is the "Chmelnitsky" massacre that few including Jews are aware of.

The "Chmelnitsky" massacre of Eastern Europe (from 1648 to 1649) reveals a barbaric treatment of the Jewish people that defies the imagination. Below describes with horrific detail what took place:

> "Some of them (the Jews) had their skins flayed off them and their flesh flung to the dogs. The hands and feet of the others were cut off, and then flung onto the roadway where carts ran over them, then they were trodden underfoot by horse...And many were buried alive, children were slaughtered in their mother's bosoms, and many children were torn apart like fish.

39

They ripped up the bellies of pregnant women, took out the unborn children, and flung them in their faces. They tore open the bellies of some of them and placed a living cat within the belly and left them alive thus, not be able to take the living cat out of the belly". 7

THE HOLOCAUST

Hitler had a solution to what he saw as the "Jewish problem." The most notorious of all plans throughout human history became known as, "the final solution." Its goal was the carefully orchestrated plan of exterminating all of European Jewry. It took 6 million Jewish lives, and of those were my paternal grandparents, uncles, aunts, and cousins.

Hitler's propaganda campaign was insidious. Claiming the "vileness of the Jews was part of their blood," he said that their race was inferior, physically, mentally, and culturally. Jews, he said, "polluted modern life with filth and disease, "and they poisoned others with germs, but somehow managed to preserve themselves."

He intensified this decease of Jewish hate in German society by creating a board game for Germans called, "Jews Get Out." This game was sold throughout Germany in 1939 and 1940. Then in 1938, a children's anti-Semitic book was published called The Poisonous Mushroom through which German children could be implanted with Jewish hate.

Jewish hate was spread further by posting public signs throughout Germany, warning women and girls to watch out for the rapist, the "Jew." Other signs said, "Beware of JEWS and pickpockets. "Then he created over four hundred laws and decrees which defined what a "non-Aryan" is: A non-Aryan was anyone descended from non-Aryan, especially Jewish parents or grandparents, even if only one parent or grandparent was a non- Aryan. Following this definition, it became official that every government worker in Germany had to prove his or her lineage. [9]

One Final Note: In the context of the historical horrors given above, understandably Judaism views Christianity through a history of great suffering. But such actions could not have come from genuinely transformed believers in our Messiah. Still, they were done in the name of Christianity.

By this history, many sectors of the Jewish community, as difficult as this may be to understand, have not encountered the love of the Cross, the symbol of life, and something synonymous with mercy and sacrifice. Instead, it has been a historical symbol of prejudice and horrific anti-Semitism. Given these dark periods, we discover a key to Jewish survival from the words of Ernest Van Den Haag in his book "The Jewish Mystique." He writes the following.

> "When the enemy is overwhelmingly stronger, when any violent resistance must end in defeat and bring even greater and more extended suffering, the only chance of survival lies in developing a large tolerance for unjust burdens, in learning to suffer without striking back. By clinging to this lesson, the Jews adapted themselves to reality and managed to survive

individually and collectively. A small powerless group surrounded by hostile and powerful masses can hope to survive only by never defying them, by not responding to challenges, by suffering mutely, by making itself as inconspicuous as possible and as useful as possible to the powers that be. Thus, at tremendous cost to their self-esteem, the Jews managed to be tolerated physically, if in no other way."

CHAPTER STUDY QUESTIONS

1. Explain the relationship of Israel to the nations from the scriptures of Isaiah 17:12 & Obadiah 1:18. In what ways does the analogy of fire and water speak to the relationship of the nations and the Jewish people.
2. What are Pogroms?
3. What is a Blood Libel? When did they first occur?
4. What are Tribunals and Crusades?
5. Describe the impact of the Holocaust in witnessing to Jewish people?

    a. What explanation can you give of an all Loving God that would allow it?
6. What did Hitler call his plan to exterminate all of European Jewry?

CHAPTER THREE

Into the Melting Pot

THOUGH AMERICA WAS FOUNDED UPON THE JUDEO CHRISTIAN BELIEF, AND RELIGIOUS freedom, it was not without anti-Semitism. Certainly not unique from other states in America, in a New Jersey town where I have lived for the last forty years, and my wife twenty years before me, a sign was posted by a lake community decade earlier that said; No blacks, No dogs, No Jews. Yes, though America became a "Melting Pot," a place for all cultures and people, anti-Semitism was here.

The term "Melting Pot" is believed to come from a Jewish man in England named Israel Zangwill, a playwright that identified with the same understanding as Theodor Herzl when he created his portrayal of a Zionist state. In 1896 Herzl published a work called The Jewish State, in it he posed these alternatives: "Jews should choose either national existence in Palestine or assimilation; they should finally reorganize themselves, normalize and become like everyone else." [1]

Zangwill's drama of The Melting Pot in 1914, portrayed an interfaith couple, Jewish and Christian, as a means of ending the most considerable dissimilarity among Americans. Zangwill saw the New World as more glorious than Rome or Jerusalem because America is the place where "all races and nations come to labor and look forward to." 2

LET'S GO to AMERICA

When we think of Jewish history in America, how it evolved and what their early struggle was like, one lesser-known fact revolves around how it began. This Jewish history in America is a compelling case and point — was it misfortune or fate that brought these early Jewish settlers to America?

In April of 1654, sixteen ships were readying to set sail in the harbor of Recife, Brazil. Aboard were one hundred and fifty Jewish families, mostly children of some of the Marranos that had fled the Spanish and Portuguese Inquisition and had settled in Brazil. Again, forced to convert and embrace the Roman Catholic religion or leave the country, they chose to sell their homes, their possessions and set out on the high seas for land where religious freedom was possible. But their first intention was not America.

Of these sixteen ships, the St. Charles with twenty Jewish passengers aboard was looted by pirates at sea and had lost all of their money and possessions, and now unable to complete their journey to Holland called Old Amsterdam at the time and also my birthplace. The captain of the ship, unsympathetic to their misfortune and wanting payment, immediately diverted his ship from their original destination to New Amsterdam, which later became become known as Manhattan Island. He intended to have the Jews arrested as soon as they took a dock.

But miraculously, if it were not for the kindness of a captain of a French vessel who captured the pirates and recovered the Jew's money and belongings, they would have indeed been imprisoned. 3

Despite these early difficulties, time and experience would see Jewish immigration gain significant momentum. In the mid to late 1700s, and by 1820, an estimated six thousand Jews were already living in America. But when it comes to early America and the Jew, the first settlers viewed the Jews with a sense of ambivalence. This prejudice was because Jews were seen as different from the others.

Early American settlers were mainly farmers and ranchers, and strong, hard-working people. But they misunderstood the Jews because they were known as "people of the city;" principally business people and artisans. The Jews worked as hard, and they just channeled their efforts differently. Nevertheless, the Jews were seen as reaping the fruits of others hard labor.

More central, however, was the fact that the early settlers saw America as a new Christian nation, and the Jews viewed as "Christ-killers," a label carried over from former England. Therefore, Jews were as people that needed rehabilitation. Of course, this was always remedied by conversion to Christianity. Jews were even banned from voting in early colonial America until New York became the first state to allow them to vote. Soon after, the rest of the colonies followed their lead. Still, the attitudes and prejudices continued to characterize the early American frontier for the Jew.

PEOPLE AND PLACES
Of INTEREST

Another distinction between the early settlers and the Jews was the fact that the gentiles that arrived in pre-colonial times were not fleeing a homeland marked by persecution as the Jews. Therefore, gentiles could always return to their homeland if things became too difficult, but not the Jews. Though some Jewish families prospered greatly, most of the early Jewish settlers were extremely poor, and they were always viewed as strange due to their religious tradition.

Such early anti-Jewish sentiment is brought to light in a letter by Peter Stuyvesant, the governor of New Amsterdam. On September 22, 1654, he petitioned the Dutch West India Company, who was his employer, to rid his new island of the Jews. Thankfully the Dutch West India Company had large investors who were Jewish, so they opposed his appeal. But Stuyvesant still sought to make the Jews feel unwelcome. He called them repugnant, deceitful, enemies, and blasphemers of Christ. He even went as far as to refer to them as "Christ Killers." In His appeal he wrote the following,

> "We have for the benefit of this week and newly developing place and the land in general, deemed it useful to require them (the Jews) in a friendly way to depart; also praying most seriously in this connection, for ourselves as also for the general community of your

47

worships, that the deceitful race—such hateful enemies and blasphemers of the name of Christ—be not allowed to further infect and trouble this new colony...[4]"

In Boston where the Puritans settled, they thought for sure that they were the real Jews and genuine heirs of the promises that God made in the Hebrew Bible. Three generations after the beginning of the northern colonies, Samuel Willard outlined Puritan sentiments in a sermon that he preached in 1700. "...The Jews were scorn and reproach to the world: "...the happy day of the conversion could improve their condition." [5] The Puritans saw the "end of days" upon them, and they believed the second coming could not happen unless most Jews were converted.

Hannah Adams, a descendant of Henry Adams and a distant cousin of John Adams, published a work on the history of the Jews in 1812. In her view of history, the suffering of the Jews is due to their rejection of Christ. Adams accuses the Jews of continuing to regard themselves as "the chosen people" and "superior to all others." [6]

Hanna Adams believed what was the general view in America, that American freedom for the Jew was an opportunity for them to be converted and enlightened, which was always Christianity. Later that same Hanna Adams wrote in 1812, "The United States is perhaps the only place where the Jews have not suffered persecution, but have, on the contrary, been encouraged and indulged in every right as citizens."

A view into Thomas Jefferson's life also reveals ambivalence toward the Jews: "They should labor to achieve equality in

48

science that is in secular learning so that they will become objects of respect and favor." 7" Later, he was more favorable toward them and their religious rights, especially after the Bill of Rights and the Constitution. Thomas Jefferson was, in fact, the one who incorporated the principle of separation of church and state into the Constitution. He said, "building a wall of separation between church and state, and that religion is a matter solely between a man and God." [8]

Finally, there is the automaker and industrialist Henry Ford who was the major trumpet of anti-Semitism in his day. The Protocols of the Elders of Zion published a generation earlier and most likely by the secret police of the Russian czar, was aimed at justifying anti-Semitic policies, and was published in the United States in 1919. Henry Ford financed the production of hundreds of thousands of copies. The publication asserted that the Jews were part of a conspiracy to dominate the world. On this basis, Ford's paper became the leading voice of anti-Semitism in America in the 1920s.

INSTITUTIONS OF HIGHER LEARNING

Education always being essential to the Jewish people, entering prominent institutions of higher learning, particularly before the early 1920s, went mostly unhindered. However, a growing number of universities began to feel uneasy with an increasing Jewish presence as Jews began to outperform their gentile classmates. Universities started to institute quotas in places like Harvard, Princeton, and Yale.

Consider the words from Harvard President A. Lawrence

Lowell in 1922; "If every college in the country would take a limited proportion of Jews, we should go a long way toward eliminating race feeling amongst our students." Lowell was later forced to retract his statement, but Jewish enrollment was mysteriously curtailed sharply after the incident.

At Yale, there was a decision that students should be admitted on the basis of character rather than just scholarship. Dean Frederick Jones at Yale University found that a Jew won almost every single scholarship of any value. He stated, "In terms of scholarship and intelligence, Jewish students led the class, but their characteristics make them markedly inferior." Of course, this so-called inferiority could only be remedied by conversion to Christianity. [9]

When it came to Medicine, Medical schools discouraged Jewish enrollment through Jewish quotas that forced thousands of Jews to go abroad for medical training. During the turn of the century, gentiles controlled virtually all hospitals as well as the entire medical profession. For Jews, it was practically impossible for them to join a hospital staff or find a Jewish professor in an American medical school. Consequently, the field was virtually closed to Jewish students seeking medical degrees.

DARK MOMENT IN JEWISH AMERICAN HISTORY

Perhaps one of the darkest moments in Jewish history in America was when Leo Frank, the only Jew hanged America, was falsely accused of killing a young girl named Mary Phagan on August 17, 1915, in Marietta, Georgia. After being condemned to live in prison, Frank was brought to prison to serve his sentence. But an unrelenting public wanting vengeance organized themselves into a group called the "Knights of Mary Phagan."

They then drove to the prison, where they forcefully removed Frank from his cell and brought him back to Marietta, where they hung him from a tree until dead. Leo Frank was the only known Jew ever lynched on American soil. This case was so sensationalized; stores sold out of rope because people began carrying lengths of rope as memorabilia. Branches of the tree where Frank hung were cut down and kept as souvenirs. It was this incident in Jewish American history that caused the Anti-Defamation League of the B'nai B'rith to be established.

In 1982, nearly seventy years later, a man known as Alonzo Mann volunteered that he had seen a man named Jim Conley carrying Mary Phagan's body at the factory where Frank worked. On March 11, 1986, Leo Frank received a posthumous pardon from the Georgia State Board of Pardons and Paroles and was declared innocent. On March 7, 2008, a historical marker was erected in front of 1200 Roswell Road in Marietta near the location where Frank was hung. 10

ANTI-SEMITISM:
A SPIRITUAL SICKNESS

Again, and again, history has demonstrated that Anti-Semitism is not a sickness of just one nation or religion, but a condition that continues to cross all creeds and nations. Multitudes of nations have sanctioned and condoned it within their borders. And in surveying the history of anti-Semitism, the question of whether that history proves unique or not is a question that remains.

Harvard psychologist Gordon Allport offered his explanation in 1953 when he attributed anti-Semitism to an illness. He stated in his book, The Nature of Prejudice," prejudiced people are psychologically abnormal." [11] Consequently, his published thought on anti-Semitism pronounced Jew-haters as sick. But this was simply an easy rationalization for Jewish hatred. Anti-Semitism is a spiritual sickness. It is a grave error than to attribute it to a psychological illness since it is birth in the dark-spiritual-realm that is rooted in a sinister conspiracy to destroy the elected of God.

Make no mistake. Anti-Semitism points to a deep spiritual struggle. In Ephesians chapter six, Paul provides the reason for every human conflict, including anti-Semitism. Though it speaks about the body of believers and their interaction with one another in general terms, every social conflict is spiritually rooted. When it comes to the Jewish people and Israel, it is a hotbed of contention in the spiritual realms.

SATAN'S DARK PAST

Longer than creation itself, a dark plot has been looming over God's plan for the Jewish people. From the eternities of time, or the dateless past, satan fell, and war raged between Lucifer and God (Isaiah 14: 13-15.) It was not much of war, really! It took place over a heart change in Lucifer to be as God, and to be God. This cataclysmic fall only took a moment. Maybe it was a second. How long does it take to sin in one's mind and heart?

For satan, this rebellion finished his time with God, and no longer would he walk the stones of fire that encircled the throne — No longer would he hold the position of head Cherub and facilitate God's activities in both Heaven and earth. This first war, between God and Lucifer, would form the quintessential spiritual struggle against God's ways and His design for planet earth. And this is where the elected of God, the Chosen People, the Jewish people, come in. Let's recall the fact that satan revealed his desire to be King over the earth and establish his government, to sit where David sat, and where Yeshua will sit in the future.

In a subsequent chapter, we will elaborate upon satan's world view, and understand how it is connected to his long-held desire to destroy the Jew. Still, make no mistake, anti-Semitism is a spiritual malady. It is a disease of Jewish hate that can only be cured by one's spiritual rehabilitation, only through the redeeming power of the Messiah. But once anti-Semitism is recognized for the spiritual sickness that it is, then and only then can one begin to understand satan's real vision:

A world without the Jew, and a future temple with his name inscribed upon it.

SATAN'S WAR

Throughout this war, satan has had many self-inspired moments to take worship from God. One surrounded the festival of Chanukah when Antiochus ordered an altar to Zeus erected in the Temple. He ordered pigs to be sacrificed at the altar of the Temple. This provoked a Jewish revolt led by the Maccabees of which we observe in the festival of Chanukah.

When it comes to the end of days, the anti-Christ, like the former Antiochus, will again force worship away from the One True God. Always he is seeking to receive worship from all people, rich or poor, (Revelation 13.) Satan has long wanted to be worshipped as God, but this will never occur. Listed below is the only recorded account in scripture of satan's rebellion against God. It forms the foundation for Jewish hate throughout both human and Christian church history,

> "How art thou fallen from heaven, O Lucifer, son of the morning? how art thou cut down to the ground, which didst weaken the nations! For thou hast said in thine heart, I will ascend into heaven, / I will exalt my throne above the stars of God:/ I will sit also upon the mount of the congregation, in the sides of the north: I will ascend above the heights of the clouds; I will be like the Most High." (Isaiah 14:12-14)

END OF CHAPTER QUESTIONS

1. Who was Leo Frank and what Jewish organization was formed as a result?
2. Can you describe Anti-semitism? And where is it rooted?
3. What are the Protocols of the Elders of Zion? Who in American history was a primary financier of it, and helped distribute it throughout America?
4. Where did the first Jews settle, and where did they come from?
5. Describe the root cause of antiSemitism?
6. Where in Scripture can you demonstrate Satan's ajenda to destroy the Jew?   Explain why?

CHAPTER FOUR

Laws of Zion
"Biblical Principles of Jewish Survival"

SOLIDLY ESTABLISHED IN SCRIPTURE ARE ENDURING PRINCIPLES, of what I term Laws of Zion. The cause of Jewish survival is found here that goes back as far as 3800 years ago when God first spoke with Abraham. They also form one monolithic truth. What is a monolith?

Typically, a monolith is a solid geological mass that is found on the side of a mountain that is usually laid bare through erosion. For our purposes, it is compared to a mountain of Biblical truths pertaining to Israel and the Jewish people that are being laid bare today due to new light being shed on old truths. Eroding today are anti-Jewish theologies, thinking, mindsets, and traditional tenets that have long concealed the reality of Israel and her relationship to the Church and the Last Days. This is only possible through the power and work of the Holy Spirit.

FIVE SPIRITUAL LAWS OF ZION

Presented five of these laws or principles, which I compare to such seen and unseen natural principles that keep order in our own material universe. Consider the law of gravity or the law of aerodynamics. Gravity, for example, is the force that pulls an object toward the center of the earth — what goes up must come down. Aerodynamics, and its principles can be witnessed when an airplane remains airborne, yet you cannot detect the wind flowing over its wing on an exact angle that enables an aircraft to get the lift.

When it comes to Israel and the Jewish people, many cannot understand how and why the Jewish people have survived or how Israel was reborn in 1948. But they have! The Jewish people now live in their land of Biblical history owed simply to unseen Biblical Laws and principles. These principles establish a self-evidencing truth that keeps order in a spiritual and prophetic universe.

◆ ◆ ◆

[1]. Law of the Covenant: The first of these laws is the **"Law of the Covenant,"** specifically, the Abrahamic covenant where the actual promise that God made to Abraham is found. This law is reinforced in our study by what is called "terms of power."

[2] Divine Law Enforcement: The second is the principle of **"Law Enforcement."** God enforces the covenant with a well of untold promises and assurances of Jewish survival; "For

God is not as a man that he should lie, and what He states, He shall do, and make it good" (Numbers 23:19 KJV.)

[3] Law of Divine Preservation: In the third law, we see people who have a rare ability to rise out of the harshest of circumstances; **"The Law of Preservation."**

[4] Angel of the Lord: In the fourth, we meet the **"Angel of the Lord;"** a divine messenger and facilitator of God's word. He is also the one who encamps about Israel and the Jewish people.

[5] The law of His Namesake: Finally, the fifth law teaches us that everything God does, He does for His "Name's Sake," **"The Law of His Namesake".** Israel endures because it concerns the honor of His Great Name.

1st

LAW OF ZION

(The Principle of Covenant)

As one might expect, the survival of the Jewish people comes from the covenant. God's testament also poses dangerous consequences for nations whose treatment and attitude towards the Jew is unpleasing to God.

The covenant, particularly since the "One True God" covenanted with Abraham, then with Isaac, and later Jacob portrays Israel as the only nation that is bound by this covenant with the One True God. God speaks to Abram and shows him the land, "All the land that you see I will give to you and your offspring forever." Also, "go walk through the length and breadth of the land, for I am giving it to you" (Genesis 13:15-17.)

Hence, God gave to the Jewish people and their generations a description of the Promised Land that remains the basis of Genesis 15:18-21, and its signing ceremony in Genesis 17:1-8. God also reminded them that it was "His" land in Leviticus 25:23-24, a property that He would allow them to enter in as "stewards." We will expound further on this notion of "steward" later in this chapter.

When God reminded the second-generation nation of Israel of their special covenant relationship with Him in what is the land aspect of the covenant, Moses, Joshua, and Caleb, from the first generation that came out of Egypt and wandered for 40-year's, are standing at the Jordan River ready to cross (Deuteronomy 29: 2-3, 10-15.) And since the covenant is like a permanent trust, if any generation determined to obey its conditions, they retrieve the fuller and complete blessings and promises that the first generation lost. This provision is for every generation!

In review of the covenant, I take a legal perspective because of its legal nature. I Liken the Abrahamic Covenant to the bulwarks of our civil liberties. It seems intuitive to me to compare it to such documents as, The Constitution of the United States, the Bill of Rights, or the Declaration of Independence. All of them form pillars upon which society rests. The Abrahamic covenant forms the bulwarks of how the Jew was to live as God ordained them, and what the nations were to respect and obey also.

To illustrate these principles of God's dealings with Abraham, we want to bring the spiritual nature of God's covenant into the natural, as the spiritual always manifests' its reality in the natural. We do this trough "power terms" that undergird the principles of the Covenant God's devotion to Israel.

TERMS OF POWER

1st

POWER TERM

DECLARATION

The first term, Declaration, denotes how God created everything. The second term is Self-evidence, and it defines its truth. The third is the well-known term Inalienable, which in the context of our study states that no human agency holds power and authority over a person's rights; this speaks of an individual as well as an individual nation.

When it comes to the term, declare, we often find it in the King James Version to mean saith. It conveys the idea of a divine utterance delivered to man, as when the Israelites sought the direction of Adonai through the Urim and Thummim" and the Ephod of the high priest 2 (I Samuel 23:9; 30:7-8; 2 Samuel 16:23; I Kings 6: 16.)

The term "declare," also establishes God's closeness to His people. From Isaiah in chapter 56:8, "The Sovereign LORD declares, "He who gathers the exiles of Israel, I will gather still others to them besides those already gathered." God said, "I declared what I would do, and then I did it –I saved you. No foreign god has ever done this before. You are my witnesses that I am the only God, "states the Lord. From eternity to eternity, I am God. No one can oppose what I do. No one can reverse my actions" (Isaiah 43: 10-13 NIV.)

On the other hand, Isaiah portrays almost a scene in a

present-day courtroom where God is testifying and declaring before Heaven and earth against His people, which can also reveal His closeness to His people, "Hear, O heavens! Listen, O earth! For the LORD has spoken: 'I reared children and brought them up, but they have rebelled against me" (Isaiah 1:2.)

Isaiah states in chapter 56:8, "The Sovereign LORD "declares" — he who gathers the exiles of Israel: "I will gather still others to them besides those already gathered. "In the New Covenant declare is equated to divine utterances or as living oracles that parallel commandments to be administered by God (Rom 3:2; Hebrews 5:12; Acts 7:38.) This again makes them unchanging and non-restrictive. Like the High Supreme Court of the United States ruling, God speaks, from the courts of Heaven. He declares, and Heaven and earth come into alignment. Consider these words; "until the His name is declared in Zion and His praise in Jerusalem and the people of the world assemble to worship the Lord" (Psalm 102:21-22.)

> Whenever God speaks, He declares something, and immediately it comes into reality. Take the first three chapters of Genesis when God began to declare His creation to come into existence, He said, "let there be water under the sky," and there was water! He declared, "let the waters teem with every living creature, and varieties of every kind filled the sea". Consider these words from both the Psalmist and the prophet Isaiah. "He sends his command to the earth; his word runs swiftly. He spreads the snow like wool and scatters the

frost like ashes. He hurls down his hail like pebbles. Who can withstand his icy blast? He sends his word and melts them; he stirs up his breezes, and the waters flow. He has revealed his word to Jacob, his laws and decrees to Israel."

(Psalm 147:15-19.)

"...Rain and the snow that falls from Heaven, but returns not so that it will give seed to the sower and bread for the eater, so is my word that goes out from my mouth: It will not return to me empty, but will accomplish what I desire and achieve the purpose for which I sent it"

(Isaiah 55:10-11.)

Stated over 400 times in Scripture, the reader can discover wonderful declarations that affirm God's devotion to the Jewish people and the land of Israel. Consider this one from Psalms 128:5-6," The Lord shall bless thee out of Zion, and thou shalt see the good of Jerusalem all the days of their life. 6. Yea, thou shalt see thy children's children and peace upon Israel." There are forty-five other passages found in the Psalms alone.

Therefore, wars, dispersions, and attempted exterminations will always fail to remove the Jewish people and Israel from the earth. God declared, "He will set Israel in praise, fame and honor high above all the nations that he has made, and that you will be people holy to the LORD your God, as he promised" (Deuteronomy 26:19.) Always and forever, Scripture will return us to Israel's historical hopes of land and the future.

"O people of Zion who live in Jerusalem, you will weep no more. How gracious he will be when you cry for help! As soon as he hears, he will answer you" (Isaiah 30:19-20.) "And you are my servant, you have been chosen to know me" (Isaiah 43: 10.) Or, "…Listen! Your watchmen lift up their voices; together, they shout for joy. When the LORD returns to Zion, they will see it with their own eyes" (Isaiah 52:8.)

2nd
POWER TERM:
SELF-EVIDENCE

When it comes to the term self-evidence, Benjamin Franklin said, self-evidence is "found through reason and is free from the Yoke of required proof of a legal theory He is speaking about our individual natural rights that are founded upon principles of natural law. With this understanding, no one needs to provide evidence of their individual right to exercise him or her because your rights are self-evident.

In the context of our study, we can demonstrate the law of Self-Evidence in the millions of believers that journey to the Holy Land each year. Why do they go? They are compelled with a burden to pray and give of their finances to the causes of Zion. These millions of pilgrims arrive because God's covenant with the Jew and the land of Israel is self-evident. This is solidly established in the Word of God. Even more Self-Evident is the fact that the Jewish people are living in their land today. All of these forms a self- evidencing truth of what Scripture has long declared.

3rd POWER TERM
INALIENABLE / UNALIENABLE

Unalienable was first made famous in the Declaration of Independence," We hold these truths to be self-evident, that all men are created equal, that they are endowed by" their Creator with certain unalienable Rights." Here, we learn how wonderfully this term wraps itself around Jewish claim to the land.

Unalienable is defined as; rights that are incapable of being alienated, sold or transferred. When thinking of this and our individual rights, which were provided to us by the Declaration of Independence, it guarantees that no one person has the power to trade or barter away their individual rights. This is particularly the case since our Creator endowed those rights to us. You see, the prefix "un," cancels something within that word. For instance, being un-able means that one does not have a certain ability for a particular task. Unworthy simply means one who is not worthy. Or we see this in the difference between being ungracious to someone that ingratiates himself to another. In the case of the word unalienable, the "lien" is canceled.

Let's go further.

In doing additional research for this chapter, I consulted Black's Law Dictionary, sixth edition, Page 1523. Unalienable is defined as something that is incapable of being sold and transferred." An added meaning comes from the original understanding of English Common Law, which the United States and most Commonwealth countries are heirs to, "land cannot be given away, sold, or granted to another…the land can only be inherited. Thus, it moves from one generation to the next." This understanding brings us closer to what God intended when He covenanted with Abraham.

Thomas Jefferson's experiences with unalienable was historic. When he submitted the original draft of the Declaration of Independence, he employed the word inalienable, not unalienable. Immediately the Declaration committee was alarmed, and Thomas Jefferson found himself at odds with the Declaration Committee. To understand the conflict, we first learn that the definition of the word unalienable has changed dramatically over the course of 300 years. While today they virtually mean the same, in Colonial days, they meant the complete opposite.

Now recalling what has been previously stated on Unalienable: Inalienable gave one the right to sell their rights as well as trade them or even barters for them. This, of course, had serious ramifications for this new country 300 years ago.

Thankfully, the Declaration Committee immediately determined if God our Creator endowed these rights to man, how can one take away or give away, or even sell away, what their Creator gave? The Declaration Committee had the wording changed to unalienable in order to guard man's rights forever.

APPLYING INALIENABLE & UNALIENABLE TO ISRAEL

When it comes to Israel, it is her unalienable rights that truly define her position in the land. From our study we learned that she actually holds no lien or title to the land since the land agreement (Land Covenant) was actually God's "tenant contract" with the Jewish people.

Let's also be clear. The idea of a "tenant contract" may seem to lessen the power of God's covenant with the Jew. But this so-called "tenant contract" between God and the Jew made the Jewish people a bonded community, bound by the One True God. This agreement then is not abstract or concocted, as their enemies would assert. Always, Israel was "the" chosen steward of this vineyard that we know as Israel. Here are these words, "The land must not be sold permanently, because the land is mine, and you are but aliens, and my tenant" (Leviticus 25:23.) Consequently, Israel has always rested in this unusual and exclusive un-alienable state of being—God holds the inalienable rights, and Israel holds the unalienable rights to the land.

The famous thirteenth-century Exegete and Biblical scholar Moses Nachmanides, interprets the phrase," for the land is mine" in Leviticus 25:23, "Here God is speaking to Israel through Moses; "You are but stranger's residents with me." From two other translations, "The land must not be sold permanently, because the land is mine and you are but aliens and my tenants." (TNIV.) "And remember, the land is mine, so you may not sell it permanently. You are merely My tenants and sharecroppers" (NLT.) In conclusion, no one can own the Holy Land with any permanency other than God. [3]

Consequently, nations that seek to place conditions or attachments to the Land, which God has transferred to [His] first-born, will never turn out well. For the United States, this is significant. To the weakening of our country and the ignorance of our administration, the U.S. has undertaken actions numerous times to divide Israel for a Palestinian state, which violates both Israel's inalienable rights (the tenant,) and God's inalienable rights (the Landowner.) Let me illustrate it this way in a parable:

> A landowner was going on a long journey. He gave charge of his vineyard and his home to his servants for them to occupy, care, and protect it. But the landowner had the inalienable rights, and the power and authority to confer upon them this exclusive right to be his tenants. In turn, the servant received the unalienable rights (they're exclusive right to take possession of the vineyard.) Others heard that the landowner was away on a long journey, and they began to pressure the servants to share the owner's vineyard. They began to overrun the borders. They offered to buy some of the land, or trade for the land. But no agreement was possible because the servants only possessed the unalienable rights; they had no authority.
>
> Of course, hostility arose between the legal tenant and those wanting a portion of the landowner's vineyard.

They did not realize that wanting claim to the land with equal status as the legal tenants were violating again, both the landowner's inalienable rights and the servant's unalienable rights. Only the landowner Himself could solve this upon His return.

2nd

LAW OF ZION:

(God's Enforcement of His Covenant)

As the One might expect, the survival of the Jewish people comes from the covenant. God's testament also poses dangerous consequences for nations whose treatment and attitude towards the Jew is unpleasing to God. But God speaks to Abram and shows him the land, "All the land that you see I will give to you and your offspring forever." Also, "go walk through the length and breadth of the land, for I am giving it to you" (Genesis 13:15-17.).

Hence, God gave to the Jewish people and their generations a description of the Promised Land that remains the basis of Genesis 15:18-21, and its signing ceremony in Genesis 17:1-8. God also reminded them that it was "His" land in Leviticus 25:23-24, a property that He would allow them to enter in as "stewards." We will expound further on this notion of "steward" later in this chapter.

When God reminded the second-generation nation of Israel of their special covenant relationship with Him in what is the land aspect of the covenant, Moses, Joshua, and Caleb, from the first generation that came out of Egypt and wandered for 40-year's, are standing at the Jordan River ready to cross (Deuteronomy 29: 2-3, 10-15.) And since the covenant is like a permanent trust, if any generation determined to obey its conditions, they retrieve the fuller and complete blessings and promises that the first generation lost. This provision is for every generation.

As the Judiciary branch safeguards our founding father's documents, God has a judiciary that protects His covenants. He will also utilize natural events and or spiritual principalities to do so. In truth, the world was not designed to run entirely on its own. His most considerable intervention was when He sent His Son the Jewish Messiah to rescue man from himself.

Yet, throughout Biblical and Church history, God has graced the earth with glorious revivals and visitations. These come to wake up man and refresh his spirit. He has also intervened when man defies His laws as well. Consider this when it comes to the Jewish people and the message that is conveyed in Genesis 12:3: "I will bless those who bless you, and whoever curses you I will curse, and all peoples on earth will be blessed through you."

◆ ◆ ◆

What does it mean to be blessed? And what does it mean to be cursed? The passage rightfully states that the Jew sits upon an axis of cause and effect. God declares warnings or blessings to the world based upon their treatment of the Jew. Again, "those who bless Israel seem to be blessed, and those who curse Israel seem to be cursed." Without a doubt, the world has rarely considered the Jews as an extraordinary nation, while the Jews have always considered themselves to be a unique people. Both quantum points come from Genesis 12:3.

The one, the nations have long been jealous of the Jew and the blessings of God. The second, the Jew acknowledges this awareness of them, which has been reinforced by their historical experiences. Yet, despite a problematic history, most Jews accept it as real that God's affection is towards them as people. This unique realization Genesis 12:3 affirms. So regardless, deep within the Jewish psyche is an awareness that they are a people chosen by an Almighty God.

ZECARIAH'S LEGACY

To illustrate the Genesis 12:3 principles further, one can turn to the book of Zechariah, specifically to the first three chapters. We will elaborate on these Scriptures further in the next Law as well. But in chapter one, Zechariah receives an extraordinary vision on the subject of the Babylonian captivity of the Jewish people. The visions take place in heaven, but the events take place on earth (Read Zechariah chapters 1-3 to capture the entire scene.)

In this vision, horses of varied colors leave heaven. Their riders go on assignment to survey the disposition of the nations while the Jews are enduring 70 years of punishment in Babylon. To understand the significance of this mission, these horses and riders were real invisible agencies that often let go of the glories of heaven to complete an assignment. Also, leading this mission is none other than the Second Person of the Godhead, Yeshua Himself. He is the One riding the red horse, the one that the prophet saw by night riding a red horse and accompanied with other riders on red, speckled, and white horses.

Who were they?

"These are they the LORD hath sent to walk to and fro through the earth" (Zechariah 1:10.) KJV "Further, any time the Father sends His First-born Son to do something, you know it is important!

Shown throughout this passage is the Man standing amid the myrtle trees which is the Angel of the Lord and is also the man riding upon the red horse. Then in chapter six, His identity is finally revealed as the "Branch". Other passages refer to the [Son] as the Branch as well; Zechariah 6:12; Jeremiah 33:15; 23: 5; Isaiah 11:1). The Talmud also confirms that this man is the Second person of the God Head, "This Man can refer to none but the Holy One blessed to be. He, as it is written, the Lord is a man of war" (Sanhedrin 93 a.)

♦ ♦ ♦

As this scouting team returns from earth to give their report, God utters these words: "I am very jealous for Jerusalem and Zion, but I am very angry with the nations that are at ease. I was only a little angry, but they added to the calamity "(Zechariah 1:14-15.) Babylon, along with other nations, were often appointed to punish and discipline Israel, but never to exterminate or exact unusual cruelty or go beyond what they had been commissioned to (Jeremiah 27, 28.) Further, the phrase noted in the Zechariah passage, "they that are at ease," denotes arrogance. Zechariah reveals that God takes notice of arrogant nations and their attitude towards the Jewish people.

In sum, the Zechariah passage establishes a timeless truth:

When the Jewish people suffer at the hands of the nations, God is not only angered; it brings consequences to the nations. I have often wondered if similar missions were sent out from Heaven during the Holocaust. Consider recent US Presidents who have attempted to divide the land of Israel in exchange for a Palestinian State and its consequences.

EYE TO EYE

In a book by William Koenig, published as far back as 2006 called Eye to Eye, 1 he chronicles daily real-time activity of Genesis 12:3 in relation to the United States policy on the Middle East, particularly to the dividing of Israel. He correlates the dramatic events of natural disasters that have taken place, particularly in the United States, with Presidential policy on the land of Israel. Koenig's work covers the period from 1991 to 2005. But certainly, in recent years, 2008 to the present, this principle has been exploded out to reveal unprecedented economic upheaval and natural disasters. The Obama administration has shown unprecedented degrees of stubbornness against Israel when compared to recent administrations. These will surely intensify and move America to ruin as long as this administration violates the supernatural laws of Zion, which are merely Biblical enforcements of God's covenant with Israel.

"Eye to Eye," cites 57 catastrophes, which will never be forgotten. Two of the most memorable and terrifying events was the attack upon the World Trade Towers and hurricane

74

Katrina. Koenig asks the question, what do these major record-setting events have in common?

- The ten costliest insurance events in U.S. history
- The twelve costliest hurricanes in U.S. history
- Three of the four largest tornado outbreaks in U.S. history.

The two largest terrorism events in U.S. history, and all of these major catastrophes, began or occurred on the very same day or within 24 hours of U.S. presidents Bush, and Clinton, pressuring Israel to trade her land for promises of peace and security; sponsoring "land for peace" meetings, making major public statements pertaining to Israel's covenant land, and calling for a proposed Palestinian state. Is each one of these major record-setting events just a coincidence or awe-inspiring signs that God is actively involved in the affairs of Israel? Examples from his book as the attack on the World Trade Center in 2001 and hurricane Katrina, reveals the importance of God's unchangeable promises that continue to function in the interests of God's covenant land and people." "EYE-EYE" has become one of many works today that continues to collect and correlate data on United States policy on the Middle East. This data merely reinforces what God's people have known, and what our politicians are naïve or just unwilling to realize: Whenever nations transgress God's laws, particularly regarding Israel, disasters will follow.

TONY BLAIR

When Prime Minister Tony Blair stepped down on June 27, 2007, to become Middle East Envoy, he began to lead the UK to help international efforts to divide Israel and create a Palestinian state. In the context of our study, many are discovering that there is no coincidence to England's worst flooding in her history one-month following; "Britain is suffering its worst flooding in living memory, leaving tens of thousands of people without power or water; http://news/sky.com/skynews/Home/Sky-News.

PRESIDENT GEORGE W. BUSH

In 2001 in the United States, President George W. Bush became President and served two terms. He was the first President in recent administrations that was so emboldened and determined to divide the land of Israel. Certainly, the current administration under President Obama has dwarfed Bush's efforts in this regard, and the country has suffered consequences that have dwarfed those that took place in 2007. Many during President George W. Bush's tenure believed his political motivation to divide the land of Israel was to go down in history as a President of peace rather than war. One should read the letter that is provided in Appendix III from Gershon Salomon Chairman of the Temple Mount and Land of Israel Faithful Movement Jerusalem, which was delivered to President George W. Bush during his administration.

Reflect for a moment on the natural disasters in the United

States that are provided below, particularly in 2007, when increasing pressure was on to divide Israel. It should be noted and stressed again and again that the United States has been pummeled beyond one's imagination during our current administration. Obama's idea of Israel returning to their pre-1969 borders is reprehensible, and he will continue to steer America into a collision course with more judgments to follow, as already noted.

♦ ♦ ♦

Here are some of the extreme weather events that the United States experienced during President George W Bush's tenure: 1 billion in crop damage was sustained when exceptional late March warmth led to early maturation of plants that were killed when a record April cold snap hit a large portion of the country, from the central Plains to the Southeast.

More than 2,500 new daily record high-temperature records were set in August across the central and southeastern United States. Severe to exceptional drought affected most of the Southeast that has continued from midsummer to date, affecting crops, leading to water sharing tension and ongoing water use restrictions. Drought has affected the West, parts of the upper Midwest, and parts of the Northeast. Five southeastern states, two Western states, and three mid-Atlantic and New England states declared states of emergency due to drought.

Death and millions of dollars in damages followed a series of strong storms from Texas to Kansas and Missouri in June and

July. Making matters worse were the remnants of Tropical Storm Erin, which produced heavy rainfall in the same region in August. 9 million acres burned as wildfires, fueled by heat and drought, raged across the Western United States, destroying homes and leading to several deaths. 15 named tropical storms formed in the Atlantic Basin, four more than the long-term average. Six of them were hurricanes, including Dean and Felix, which made the first back-to-back Category 5 landfalls in recorded history.

EXCERPT'S FROM MY DIARY

In 2007, I personally began to journal U.S. policy and activities as a simple exercise to correlate the US policy on Israel, and its consequences upon America; much has happened since for sure. But below is one excerpt in particular that took place on April 21, 2007:

"President George W Bush and Condoleezza Rice are once again pressuring Israel for a Palestinian State. This week we had some of the worst flooding's in the United States. Forecasted for the 2007 hurricane season are already two hurricanes, possibly three with category 5 strength. I see God's unchangeable promises again, continuing to function in the interests of God's covenant land and people.

Oh, that salvation for Israel would come out of Zion, then the LORD would restore the fortunes of his people, and Jacob will rejoice and Israel. Scripture upon Scripture, promise upon Promise, God has ensured the survival of the covenant land

and people he calls the Apple of His Eye." (See the end of chapter references for the many promises that comprise the Laws of Zion.)

OBAMA ADMINISTRATION

During the first Obama Administration, virtually no one could have imagined the natural catastrophes as well as the economic earthquakes that have occurred. No one could have imagined the catastrophes of fires in California in 2017, the devastating hurricanes as well in that year.

But going back a little, and as a backdrop to our domestic problems, the United Nations met during the week of September 20, 2012, to actually consider a membership application by the Palestinians. This act, if approved, will bring certain empowerment for future statehood. It is a blinding notion. However, that will keep natural and economic destruction insight not just for America, but the world's cooperating nations.

As some consider this platform a measure of progress, it is perverse in the context of God's Word, particularly when Palestinian statehood is derived from dividing the Promised Land. A quick look at the situation in the world today undoubtedly reveals a disquieting alarm in believers and unbelievers alike, particularly an Iran armed with nuclear weapons. As believers, we see continuity between the economic shaking and the prophetic curve that we are on. This is attributed to the closeness of the Messiah's coming.

According to scripture, a new world economy with a new

currency must emerge. For this to occur, all former economic structures, administrations, and yes, currencies must falter. Rapidly, these traditional economies are disintegrating. In such a context, policies against Israel only exacerbate the suffering and destruction of the world.

Consider President Obama's tenure in the context of US policy on Israel, and its connection to natural disasters: Only in the first half of 2011 there was $ 16.4 billion of damage due to "Thunderstorm Loss." Hurricane Irene, though its damage to land and the economy will cost less than initial estimates, it will still run $ 7 to 13 billion. The lower Mississippi River experienced the worst flooding since 1927, with economic losses estimated at $ 2 billion. According to the Texas Forest Service, 250 of the 254 counties in Texas are considered "burn bans," where all outdoor burning is prohibited. In April and June, Texas had 12 major fires that destroyed over 200 homes totaling over 50 million dollars in damages. In 2012, the summer saw 75% of America in drought conditions completely destroying corn and soy crops. Entire farms, third and fourth generation agricultural families wiped out, while millions of heads of cattle had to be destroyed.

Again, given the hour that we are in, and adding the unsavory policies of our leaders in dealing with Israel, America is headed for one disaster upon another. No doubt, scientists will attribute many natural disasters to thinning ozone layers and or natural cyclical events, and many politicians will remain ignorant of their legislative powers in relation to Israel.

Governments continue to fail to grasp the nature of the Genesis 12:3 principles, which the people of God understand well, and for this reason, we pray. But those who are overly ambitious in dividing Israel set their nation on a collision course with disaster.

When considering the current Obama administration's attitude on Israel again, reflect on a NEWSMAX on July 26, quoting former U.N. Ambassador John Bolton, who calls Barack Obama "the most hostile president" toward Israel since the Jewish state was created. He notes further Obama's early speeches, "in which the President suggested Israel should be confined to the boundaries established following the 1967 Arab-Israeli conflict known as the Six-Day war. President Obama should take note of the attitude during the Ford years. In a White House press release of President Ford's toast to Prime Minister Rabin in September 1974, he said,

> The American people have a great deal of understanding and sympathy and dedication to the same kind of ideals that are representative of Israel. And, therefore, I think we in America have a certain rapport and understanding with the people of Israel... We have mutual aims and objectives. We have the kind of relationship that I think, if expanded worldwide, would be beneficial to all mankind.

Special Note: With our current Presidential Administration, a new wave of favor rests between Israel and the United States. Time, however, will determine the full weight of its legacy.

Many term President Trump as a modern-day Cyrus. For this, we are hopeful. Time will tell!

3RD

LAW OF ZION:

(The Angel of The Lord)

John 1:2 states that Yeshua was the Word, and the Word was with God and was God. His activity, therefore, stretches into dateless past, the spiritual, and natural realm. Further, before He came to earth, He has been observed several times as the Angel of the Lord.

In this third law, we offer more detail on his role in protecting Zion. The Angel of the Lord has appeared to Joshua as the commander of the army of the LORD with his sword drawn in his hand (Joshua 5: 13-15.) To John in Revelation 6:2, "He" was with a bow and crown. In Revelation 19:9-10 He is revealed when "He" accepts Joshua's prostrate worship, (angels refuse to be worshiped.) There He declared the ground to be holy and only things, and places that are set aside for God are claimed by Him to be holy (Exodus 3:5.)

The Angel of the Lord is seen when He found Hagar near a spring in Genesis 16:7. He also wrestled with Jacob in Genesis 32:30. Jacob records that he saw God face to face. The prophet Hosea in chapter 12:4, mentions the Angel of the Lord, and in Daniel 3:25, the Angel of the Lord was the fourth man in the furnace who is described as "The Son of God" (KJV translation.) In Judges 2:1, the Angel of the Lord is mentioned as the one who brought the Israelites out of Egypt and spoke to the Israelites in verse 4. He sat under the tree in Opera in 6:11, received sacrifices and worship in 13:20, the One who could not give his name due to its holiness, and in 13:6 He came to the wife of Manoah, the father of Samson.

Referred to 25 times by Moshe (Moses) and over 60 times in the Old Testament, the Angel of the Lord had the power to forgive sins according to Exodus 23:20. Therefore, He is none other than the second person of the Divine God Head appearing in His pre-incarnate state. It should also be noted that the Exodus passage of 23:20 is a source of controversy in Judaism because, in their view, it endangers the unity of God by implying there are two powers in heaven. But this is because their understanding is still veiled to their Messiah, and they cannot grasp the concept of the Triune nature of God.

This same understanding is recorded in the Talmud, where He is compared with their Messiah because it is said, "He spent part of his existence incarnated on Earth." (Sanhedrin 35a) He is called Metator," meaning the defender of the rights of Israel. It further states that His numerical value is that of the "Almighty," and His name is also Metatron, which is derived from Metathronos, meaning "He who is enthroned by God." He is compared with Messiah because it is said, "He spent part of his existence incarnated on Earth."

Zechariah, for sure, stands out from all the other prophets in the way he writes about the "Angel of the Lord." In the first chapter of Zechariah, we see Yeshua leading an expedition out of heaven, and also the one riding upon a red horse. We see

Him also standing in the midst of a shady myrtle-grove; the red horse calls to mind the blood of war, the fury of divine jealousy, and the rage and anger for Zion's sake.

Again, and again, the fact that Messiah Himself leads this expedition is significant. Heavenly messengers often let go of the glories of heaven for God's purposes as these. We see this in the sixth chapter, and further, "He," The Angel of the Lord, Yeshua, is identified as the "Branch." Scripture often refers to the [Son] as the "Branch" (Jeremiah 33:15, 23:5, Isaiah 11:1, and 4:2.)

THE ACCUSER STEPS FORWARD

As we go back to the vision at hand, Joshua or Yehoshua represent Israel in this most extraordinary scene. They stand before the Lord God Himself when satan is also present as the accuser of the brethren. This incident is only found in this passage. Here, satan steps into the representative place of power and deity, which is the right side.

> "Then he showed me Joshua the high priest standing before the angel of the LORD, and Satan standing at his right side to accuse him. The LORD said to Satan, "The LORD rebukes you, Satan! The LORD, who has chosen Jerusalem, rebukes you! Is not this man a burning stick snatched from the fire?"
>
> (Zechariah 3:1-2 NIV.)

One can reference more passages to see that the right side is always connected with the place of honor, power, and majesty, as in the following, (Psalm 16:11, Psalm 110:5, Psalm 118:16, Exodus 15:6.) Always, the right was reserved for the Son (Luke 20:42, Acts 2:25, Romans 8:34). For this reason, Satan is always seeking to usurp the authority of the Father by taking the position of deity. When we see "the" Man (Messiah) standing among His people, symbolized by a lowly myrtle tree, He is revealing Himself as the living eternal guardian and intercessor (Zechariah 1:13; Hebrews 7:25.)

During this vision of Zechariah, satan learns that a remnant of Israel will arise out of the end-time furnace of persecution. And though great suffering will come upon them, speaking of the Jewish people in the latter days, his plan to destroy will completely fail. The enduring message of Zechariah is that the Son of God has come to earth on Zion's behalf long before 2,000 years ago as He will come again as the captain of the host. This time He will be riding on a white horse as the one faithful and true" (Revelation 19.) It establishes God's long-held devotion to Zion, revealing as well His concern for the gentile's treatment of the Jew, God's firstborn.

QUESTIONS FOR TODAY

When terrorism strikes or the Middle East is thrust into upheaval as it is taking place today, or when rising oil prices send shock waves throughout the economy, and our personal finances are affected, do our hearts remain steadfast on behalf of Zion and the Jewish people? The Jerusalem Post, j post.com, on April 29, 2010, commented on the dramatic rise of Jewish hatred and anti-Semitism as follows:

"The past year has seen a marked rise of anti-Semitism, increasing over 100 percent throughout the world, the Stephen Roth Institute for the Study of Contemporary Anti-Semitism and Racism of Tel-Aviv University outlined on Sunday, on the eve of Holocaust Memorial Day. According to the institute, violent anti-Semitic attacks, ranging from vandalism and arson against Jewish targets to beatings of Jews, increased in 2009 by a startling percentage. The report underlined the severe increase in anti-Semitic attacks, specifying that 2009 displayed the highest amount of attacks recorded in over 20 years."

Repeatedly, Jews become the easy scapegoats for our economic woes and are reminiscent of what occurred in Germany during their Pre-Nazi economic struggles. This changing and the disturbing mood is not merely from hate groups or white supremacists, as some might predict.

In a survey conducted by the Boston Resurvey entitled; "Jews are blamed for Economic Crisis," by Hillel Fendel and published by Arutz Sheva, Israel National News.com May/June issue: "Nearly 25% of American non-Jews blame the Jews for a moderate amount or more for the financial crisis. Furthermore, a total of 38.4% of the non-Jews in the U.S. attribute at least some level of blame to the group."

Once again, an article from Israel today News Agency: "Jews being blamed for US financial crisis:" Popular anti-Semitic sentiment frighteningly reminiscent of the lead-up to

Nazi rule in Germany is growing in the United States in response to the current economic crisis. With a deflated Wall Street begging for a lifeline from Washington, small businesses across the country unable to secure needed loans, and average Americans being turned away by mortgage banks, many people are looking for a scapegoat." 1

In the days ahead, will America's devotion to Zion remain strong, particularly when the Jewish people become those historical scapegoats? If Iran continues on its path to nuclear armament, will the United States stand behind Israel to defend herself? Will American's grow increasingly anti-Semitic when political and economic instability embroils America in an increasing Palestinian Israel conflict?

4th
LAW OF ZION:
A PEOPLE FASHIONED FOR SUCCESS

And thou should say in thine heart, My power and the might of mine hand hath got me this wealth. But thou shalt remember the LORD thy God: for it is he that giveth thee power to get wealth that he may establish his covenant which he sware unto thy fathers, as it is this day." (Deuteronomy 8:17-18.)

Jews possess a rare ability to emerge from tyranny and social injustice. They have the tenacity to attain success under almost impossible circumstances that defines them. In our opening passage, Moses' words to the Israelites are in the context of the Abrahamic covenant. The purpose of the above passage was to show the extraordinary relationship between Jewish successes and the covenant. Here is the passage again from Young's literal translation, "And thou hast remembered Jehovah thy God, for He it [is] who is giving to thee power to make wealthy, in order to establish His covenant which, He hath sword to thy fathers as (at) this day," YLT.

No doubt, Jewish wealth and influence have become thorns in their sides throughout history, and indeed, the Jewish people fail to make the Deuteronomy connection themselves. I am, of course, speaking of those Jewish people whose eyes remain veiled to their Messiah. However, one glorious time in the future, when all Israel comes to the knowledge of their Messiah, they will, at last, understand how and why they have survived.

When it comes to this principle in Deuteronomy, Balaam in Numbers 23 and 24 had no problem seeing what the nations have struggled with, "no misfortune is seen in Jacob, no misery observed in Israel, the Lord their God is with them." Balaam realized what the world would one day come to accept, and no one could curse what God has not cursed.

ENDOWMENTS

As previously suggested, the Jewish people have risen from unprecedented degrees of tyranny and social injustice, only to become leaders in almost every field of human endeavor. This survival is nothing less than the supernatural wiring of a people.

For purposes of illustration, I wish to turn our attention to the idea of endowments. Here the idea of "innate abilities, or endowments come forth, for instance. When God instilled specific universal drives within humankind, as seen in the first book of Genesis, God-given drives became "innate abilities."

God first endowed Adam with the ability to control and conquer his environment. He said, "fill the earth and subdue it, rule over the fish of the sea and the birds of the air and over every living creature that moves on the ground" (Genesis 1:28 NIV.) With this ability to rule and to build, and it was always for Godly and ethical purposes. Man, often went his own way to develop his empires for his namesake. For the same reason the Tower of Babel was erected (Genesis 11: 6-7 NIV.) Still, a man was endowed with the power to build and to conquer.

The same principle holds with the beautiful gift of reproduction that Adam received. It states in Genesis to "be fruitful and multiply." Here a man was endowed with a beautiful and holy sexual drive. Again, man can be un-yielded to God, and this gift becomes a perversion that produces pornography, homosexuality, extramarital affairs, and sexual addiction.

◆ ◆ ◆

At last, we come to the greatest life-changing gift that has ever been offered to man: God gave man space in his heart for Him. Many call this the God Space. This space is a God-Shaped vacuum that can only be filled with the One True God, "so God created man in his image, in the image of God he created him; male and female he created them" (Genesis 1:27.)

Out of this God space, we are given, or endowed, with a hunger for a relationship with the One True God; when man is un-yielded to God in this area, he is driven to create his own "gate" to God. This is at the root of "Babylon" or the Spirit of Babylon', or the spirit of religion. "Ba" equals the gate, and "El" is a name for God. Hence, man's many created religions are being false gates to God. Of all the endowments mentioned above, three common qualities are present; They are God-given; they are irrevocable; they can all be used for righteous or unrighteous purposes. Remember, God does not take back what He gives.

So, when God makes a declaration, the creative process

begins and ends in one breath. This is the nature and power of declaration and a divine precept that we elaborated on in the Laws of Zion.

One could ask then. Has God given the Jewish people special abilities to cause success in most fields? Has He provided the impetus for them to rise upward out of the lowest places of human suffering? Were these endowments given to assure they're continued existence? Were these endowments given to place a continual reminder before the nations of the covenant people? I believe the answer to all of these questions is a resounding yes.

Again, from the Scripture earlier from Young's literal translation, "And thou hast remembered Jehovah thy God, for He it [is] who is giving to the power to make wealth, in order to establish His covenant which, He hath sworn to thy fathers as [at] this day" YLT.

ISRAEL TODAY

To consider further Jewish successes that is connected to God-given abilities. Reflect on the record of achievements of the Jewish people. Because wherever the Jews have settled, they have become vital assets and contributors to their environment. This is in light of the fact that the Jewish population is less than 1% of the world's population. Meaning, more than 99 % of the world is non-Jewish. And in the words of the Torah, "ha-m'at mikol ha-amim," Israel is "the fewest of all the nations," this small nation has prospered beyond human reason.

Consider that Israel is no longer classified as a "developing country" by the World Bank. Israel ranks as a high-income economy and is identified as one of the most global emerging markets by the Foreign Policy Magazine Globalization Index. Israel has ranked third in the industrialized world for its people holding university degrees, after the United States and Holland. Israel has the fourth largest air force in the world after the U.S., Russia, and China. In comparison to the countries surrounding her, it is the only progressive and tolerant self-government.

Further, more new companies were produced in Israel, and more Israeli companies are listed on the NASDAQ stock exchange for small promising companies than the combined countries just mentioned. Google CEO and Chairman Eric Schmidt have said that Israel is the best place in the world for entrepreneurs after the United States.

While Standard & Poor's 500 Stock Index has fallen 4 % percent over the last 5 years, the Tel Aviv Index has soared to 60% percent. Morgan Stanley Capital International decided to upgrade Israel from an emerging market to a developed market in 2010. Steve Ballmer, who runs Microsoft, has called Microsoft an Israeli company as much as an American company because of all the Microsoft teams working in Israel. Israel has 8 universities and 27 colleges, four are among the top 150 worldwide universities, and seven are in the top 100 Asia Pacific universities.

In a recent book called, "Start-Up Nation" by Dan Senor and Saul Singer. The book addresses what is called: The Trillion-dollar question: How is it that Israel, a country of just over 7.5

million, surrounded by enemies bent on their demise, produces more start-up companies than large, peaceful nations like Canada, Japan, China, India, and the U.K.? With the savvy of foreign policy insiders, Senor and Singer examine Israeli culture and government to reveal the secrets behind the world's first-ever "start-up nation." As countries across the globe restart their own economies, and as businesses try to re-energize their entrepreneurial spirit, we can all look to Israel for some impressive, surprising clues. [1]

No doubt, the scale of achievements in a country merely the size of New Jersey (roughly 11,000 square miles) is astounding! Ernest Van Den Haag, well-known social critic, public policy professor, and writer for the National Review said this of the Jews, "They have recorded more of [history,] shaped more of it, originated and developed more of it, and suffered more for it than any other people, yet Jews have changed history." 2

As one reviews the history of Jewish achievements, one cannot but sense the supernatural throughout. This brings us back to God's blessings to Abraham and his seed. Winston Churchill said, "Some people like the Jews, and some do not. But no thoughtful man can deny the fact that they are, beyond any question, the most formidable and the most remarkable race which has appeared in the world." Please refer to Appendix IV to see how Jews have blessed and benefited societies around the world.

5th
LAW OF ZION:
FOR HIS NAMES SAKE

Unlike God, man's actions are always geared towards himself. God's are always moving towards "HIS" glory and Name's Sake. Even all things pertaining to the restoration of Israel and the Jewish people are for "His" glory. This is a truism that the future glory of Zion has always been dependent upon, "For Zion's sake will I not hold my peace, and for Jerusalem's sake I will not rest, until the righteousness thereof go forth as brightness, and the salvation thereof as a lamp that burneth" (Isaiah 62:1.)

For His Names Sake, then, the Jewish people have been saved, and for the same, He manifested His might and power to deliver them. Psalms 106:8-12 states, "… He saved them for his name's sake to make his mighty power known." From the book of Ezekiel chapter 20:22, "nevertheless I withdrew my hand, and wrought for my name's sake, that it should not be polluted in the sight of the heathen, in whose sight, I brought them forth".

The prophet Ezekiel provides an abundance of Scripture that reveals the importance of God's Holy name being upheld. Chapter 39:7 states, "I will make known my holy name among my people Israel. I will no longer let my holy name be profaned, and the nations will know that I the LORD am the Holy One in Israel."

From verse 25, "Therefore, this is what the Sovereign LORD states: I will now bring Jacob back from captivity and will have compassion on all the people of Israel, and I will be zealous for my holy name. Finally, consider from the following,

> "I had concern for my holy name, which the house of Israel profaned among the nations where they had gone. "Therefore, say to the house of Israel, 'This is what the Sovereign LORD states: It is not for your sake, O house of Israel, that I am going to do these things, but for the sake of my holy name, which you have profaned among the nations where you have gone. I will show the holiness of my great name, which has been profaned among the nations, the name you have profaned among them. Then the nations will know that I am the LORD, declares the Sovereign LORD when I show myself holy through you before their eyes,"
>
> (Ezekiel 36:21-23 NIV.)

The word in Hebrew for sake is ma'an. Under most circumstances, it determines why God intervenes in the affairs of man. For example, in second II Kings 8, we read that Jehoram son of Jehoshaphat came to be king of Judah. Because he did evil in the eyes of the Lord God, for the sake of His Name, God was forced to act. When we explore this further, we see that all things pertaining to our lives and the kingdom of God on earth is in the end for His name's sake.

Throughout, Moses encounters with Pharaoh in freeing his people, was told by God, to simply tell Pharaoh, "Let My people go that they may worship me!" Worship is to exalt the name of the Lord. God will forever marshal the powers of heaven for His Names Sake. For the same, the whole earth will ultimately understand the knowledge of His glory; "as the waters cover the sea," states the prophet, so the earth will be filled with the knowledge of the Glory of God, Habakkuk chapter two.

When it comes to His promises, it is also for His Names Sake. God holds to His course in fulfilling them, particularly when it comes to Israel and the Jewish people. So, if in some way Israel could be destroyed, albeit a preposterous idea, the Word of God would be rendered impotent and no longer could we depend upon it for anything.

Therefore, the demonically inspired declarations and plots that have been made by mad leaders throughout history against Israel have failed. Israel will prevail due to His Names Sake. God said, "that only if the heavens above can be measured and the foundations of the earth below be searched out will [He] reject all the descendants of Israel because of all they have done" (Jeremiah 31:37 NIV.) Consider the following lists of future events that are all dependent upon God's Name being upheld.

- Where would King Yeshua establish His temple? (Zechariah 14: 8-9.)
- How would the nations gather in Jerusalem to worship the Lord during the Feast of Tabernacles (Zechariah14: 16?)?
- How would Israel become the head of the nations? (Deuteronomy 8:13).

- Where would the universal world government of the greater Son of David be established, and how? (2 Chronicles 6:16.)
- Who will judge the poor of the people; where would judgment take place? (Psalm 72:4; Isaiah 11:4; Ps 106:8-12.)
- When would the nations fear Him as the sun and moon endure, throughout all generations as spoken in (Psalm 72:17.)?
- How would the world believe in the Word of God or ever trust in His promises? (Psalm 119:14) "… You have laid down precepts that are to be fully obeyed."
- How would the righteous flourish and the abundance of peace endure as the moon endured? (Daniel 7:10; Matt 26:53; Hebrews 12:22.)
- What would be made of His glorious name and promises? (Habakkuk 2:14.) How would the righteous flourish and the abundance of peace endure as the moon endured? (Daniel 7:10; Matthew 26:53; Hebrews 12:22.)
- What would be made of His glorious name and promises? (Habakkuk 2.)

In Conclusion, can a man render the scriptures impotent? Let these final words of Jeremiah echo through our hearts,

> "If you can break my covenant with the day and my covenant with the night, so that day and night no longer come at their appointed time, then my covenant with David my servant—and my covenant with the Levites

who are priests ministering before me—can be broken and David will no longer have a descendant to reign on his throne. I will make the descendants of David my servant and the Levites who minister before me as countless as the stars of the sky and as measureless as the sand on the seashore."

(Jeremiah 33:20-21)

END OF CHAPTER QUESTIONS

1. Describe the Laws of Zion.

2. How does God enforce His covenant with the Jewish people?

3. Who is the Angel of the Lord?

4. What is His role in the preservation of the Jewish people?

5. Describe the power of God's name and give examples of what He does to uphold it?

6. Why have the Jewish people surivived as well as prospered throughout history?

CHAPTER FIVE

Unlocking Israel's Election

AS MANY UNDERSTAND ISRAEL'S ELECTION TODAY, MANY STILL REMAIN OUTSIDE of this understanding. Though scripture has long solved this mystery, Christian teaching has consistently leaned towards underestimating the significance of the Jewish election, and this tendency has been untrue to the facts.

A contemporary American folk philosopher unknowingly once wrote what the entire world will someday come to know, "I have a premonition that will not leave me; as it goes with Israel, so will it go with all of us." [1]

If one had the opportunity to travel back in time to visit the first believing Jewish community, we would find people who understood that they had a theological and hierological right as Jews to be Israel, that they were Israel. This can be demonstrated in many areas, but most notably, in Acts 15, the account of the Jerusalem Council. This new Jewish leadership gathered as a formative headship in a significant way. Seeking to establish Jewish life in a new spiritual reality, these early leaders gathered to interpret this new faith for the many gentiles that were coming to faith.

Should the gentiles be circumcised? What foods should

they be forbidden to eat? These, of course, were leadership issues during this historical and brief period of headship. It was that simple and yet that difficult. Hence, the first body of believers was comprised of Jewish followers living as observant Jews. Believers, or followers of the Way (Acts 24:13-14), they kept Torah, worshipped on Saturday, attended synagogue, and observed the biblical feasts of the Lord.

Following the resurrection of our Messiah, they gathered on the first day of the week, which was called the Lord's Day. This practice evolved into the Christian Sabbath, of which the Catholic Church seems to have taken claim. The point is. They gathered on Sunday as an additional day during this early period and did not forsake Saturday Sabbath either.

When unlocking Israel's election, we must move beyond the earliest Jewish community of believers, to focus on the attitudes and mindsets that developed in Institutional Christianity. Through this development, Jewish and Israel's election was essentially confiscated. We must then touch upon a couple of grave misunderstandings and blunders that occurred with early Church fathers.

HISTORICAL MISUNDERSTANDING'S

One area of misunderstanding occurred when the Jewish people were simply blamed for Yeshua's death. But by placing the death of Christ squarely upon the shoulders of the Jewish people, the Jews were labeled as "Christ-killers" for generations. Today there remain streams within Christianity that still see the Jews as "Christ Killers."

Can anyone be blamed for Messiah's death when His Heavenly Father sent Him to earth to sacrifice His life? It is good to recall that He laid down His life willingly and sacrificially. The Scriptures show that no hefty Roman soldier had to wrestle Yeshua to the ground and forcibly drag Him to the cross. They did not have to bind him hand and foot to keep him in their grasp.

No, Yeshua stretched forth his arms on that fateful day, according to Isaiah 53, and positioned his feet on that wooden beam. He didn't try to escape when the nails pierced his hands and his feet. Additionally, our Jewish Messiah came as a servant so that the Old Testament prophecies that pointed to Him would be righteously fulfilled. He willingly and voluntarily laid down his life. And no man could take this mission from him. For this reason, He stated these powerful and comforting words, "Father, forgive them, for they do not know what they are doing" (Luke 23:34.)

◆◆◆

When the Lord forgives someone, his or her sins are cast into a sea of forgetfulness never again to be recalled. It is a brand of forgiveness offered like no other because it comes from the Messiah Himself. This means that every person, Jew, Roman, or Greek, that played a role in Yeshua's arrest, suffering, and crucifixion, unknowingly played a vital role in moving God's divine plan forward.

In sum, the notion of labeling Jews as Christ Killers has

always been rooted in pure ignorance. When one reviews the words of Isaiah together with the writings of Luke, one grasps the importance of all those that played a key role in the conclusion of God's plan for the world,

> "Surely he took up our infirmities and carried our sorrows, yet we considered him stricken by God, smitten by him, and afflicted. He was pierced for our transgressions, crushed for our iniquities, and the punishment that brought us peace was upon him, and his wounds healed us. We all, like sheep, have gone astray, each of us has turned to his own way, and the LORD has laid on him the iniquity of us all. He was oppressed and afflicted, yet he did not open his mouth; he was led like a lamb to the slaughter, and as a sheep before her shearers are silent, so he did not open his mouth. By oppression and judgment, he was taken away. And who can speak of his descendants? For he was cut off from the land of the living; for the transgression of my people, he was stricken. He was assigned a grave with the wicked and with the rich in his death, though he had done no violence, nor was any deceit in his mouth. Yet it was the LORD'S will to crush him and cause him to suffer, and though the LORD makes his life a guilt offering, he will see his offspring and prolong his days, and the will of the Lord will prosper in his hand."
>
> (Isaiah 53:4-10.)

JERUSALEM DESTROYED

A second misunderstanding took place in 70 AD when the Roman army led by Titus destroyed the Temple and sacked Jerusalem, the spiritual center of Judaism at the time. What emerged in the minds of early church fathers was the historical notion that God had a change of heart towards the Jewish people, or, God no longer considered the Jewish People His covenant people, so He sent the Romans to destroy Jerusalem.

The destruction of Jerusalem and the temple in 70 AD was certainly a fulfillment of prophecy against the generation of the Jewish leadership of that day (Matthew chapter 24.) But it was never God's final word on the Jewish people and Israel. Yet, that is what the early Church fathers thought.

Early Church fathers were even blinded to the distinction that was being made between the generation that was being judged in Matthew 12, 16, and 23, and the Jewish people as a whole. In those passages, Yeshua is condemning the generation that committed the unpardonable sin (Matthew chapter 12.) These were the religious leaders that "shut the kingdom of heaven on men's faces" (Matthew 23:13 NIV.)

Further, the chapters leading up to chapter 24 culminates in a climactic conversation with His Talmidim (disciples) concerning this great judgment that would come in 70 AD by the Romans, "Do you see all these things? "I tell you the truth, not one stone here will be left on another; everyone will be thrown down." Again, Yeshua was not casting judgment on the Jewish people as a nation as Christological teaching has leaned towards.

THE ENEMY AT THE GATE

Continually we must emphasize the anti-Jewish atmosphere and belief that the early church leaned towards. With the Hebraic root no longer connected to the church, a movement began towards independent originality away from Judaism, which most church historians acknowledge.

One individual was Justin Martyr. He saw the church as the new true Spiritual-Israel. In the Epistle of Barnabas, Christians are urged to assume their role as the new Israel. Cyprian, a Catholic saint who died in AD 258, was bishop of Carthage and an important writer of his day. He insisted that because Jews have forsaken the Lord and profaned the Holy One of Israel, Christians are now those who are permitted to call God "Our Father" since He has now become ours and ceased to be theirs — the Jews [.2]

The notion that God disowned His first-born Israel, and that God's relationship with the gentile Christian church replaced, fulfilled, and completed the promises that were given exclusively to the Jews, is something that the church came to believe. They saw themselves as ascending to the place above the Jew. Soon the early Church reveled in this idea of replacement, and patterns of thinking developed into a well-known theology called "Replacement Theology," or what is known as "Supersessionism," or "Displacement theology." All carry the same idea that comes from the Latin words super (on-upon) and sedere (to sit); someone sits on the chair of another person, or a person displaces another person. [3] This theology of replacement thinking was nothing short of a demonic intrusion into the New Covenant community.

♦ ♦ ♦

Those who subscribe to this theology of Supersessionism could be called "Supersessionists." Shockingly, I was once a passive believer in it. Yes, and therein lies the miracle of this book and my life today. I did not know why I believed it, only that it was the only teaching that I received. Isn't this the case with millions of seminary students, clergy, and laypeople today? They receive only what a particular system offers. More shocking, many Jewish people see themselves as no longer Jewish once they embrace the faith of their Jewish Messiah.

But all the terms mentioned above imply that the Old Covenant with Israel has been displaced for a New Covenant, which always brings us to a new Israel, the Church. Catholic theologian John Pawlikowski in Jesus and the Theology of Israel gives a theological reconstruction whose statements are well known in Christian thought:

> "The first, which predominated Catholicism (particularly in the liturgy,) focused around the prophecy/fulfillment motif. Jesus fulfilled the Messianic prophecies of Judaism and thus inaugurated the Messianic era for which Jews had hoped and prayed throughout the centuries. Their own spiritual blindness prevented the Jews from recognizing this fulfillment in

the Christ Event. As a divine punishment for this blindness, Jews were displaced in the covenantal relationship by those baptized into the "New Israel." [4]

Supersessionism did not stay confined, it broke into other areas and fostered anti-Jewish systems of thought and interpretive reasoning. When fully developed, the early Church replaced the synagogue, the New Testament replaced the Old Testament, Sunday replaced Saturday as the official Sabbath (that is, the replacement of the fourth commandment,) and grace replaced law. But grace was stretched so far beyond its boundaries, that the Ten Commandments were rendered nearly null and void. This is common even today.

Further, the doctrine of election, the very basis for Jewish calling, developed into a gentile-orientation, which inclined generations to be anti-Semitic. Then the Biblical promises that were specifically directed to the Jewish people were re-assigned to the Church, and the Scriptures dealing with judgment and wrath were placed squarely on the shoulders of Jewish people. In the end, a system of thought and belief evolved that made people prejudiced against the Jew.

CONSTANTINE'S INFLUENCE ON ELECTION

At the onset of Constantine's Christianity, there was the notion of Political Election. That is, imperialistic Rome came to be viewed as the reign of the Davidic Messiah.5 This is understandable since Israel also saw the Messianic restoration as political and a calling to be head of the nation's—Jewish prophecy always looked forward to a government under the headship of the coming Son of David. 6But when it came to Constantine's Christianity, it did not reflect Christ's Christianity for sure.

In 312 AD, Constantine claimed to have had a vision that instructed him to fight under the name of the Christian God, along with a cross that appeared in the sky at the battle of the Milvian Bridge outside Rome. Upon the cross were purported to be inscriptions that assured his victory. Constantine converted to Christianity and later legalized it as a state religion in 380, which brought certain relief to hundreds of thousands of Christians who were experiencing horrific persecution and torture in the years prior. Trajan, when consulting Pliny, said Christians were "considered alien to the spirit of our age."

Constantine's form of Christianity did not suppress the anti-Jewish atmosphere that had already taken root. He had an aversion to Jewish modes of worship and culture that conveyed a social sense that the Jewish people were the rejected people of God; in their minds, they were. His ecclesiastical system would disown the Jewish foundation of Christianity, and then Jews wanting to accept their Messiah had to abandon their cultural heritage, give in to conversion, and take on a completely new set of holy days, including the Sabbath.

In many respects, the consequences of Constantine's

actions and edicts, the thinking and preaching of Church fathers that would follow, assured that Jewish succession in the church would be broken. As a misrepresentation of Jewish election followed, generations became anti-Semitic; something that we find ourselves confronting repeatedly. In these things, the enemy was successful.

JEWISH ELECTION AND CALLING

For a Jewish perspective on Jewish "calling" and "election," we turn to the Song of Moses Shirat Haazinu.) Outlines there is the whole history of Israel. It begins with Jewish election by God saying, "Remember the days of old, consider the years of many generations...when the Highest divided their inheritance to the nations...for the Lord's portion is His people" (Deuteronomy 32:7-9 NKJV.) This song also mentions God's favor toward Israel, saying, "He found him in a desert land...He encircled him, He instructed him, He kept him as the apple of His eye."

Then from the prophet, Amos, one more view of election comes forth. First, Amos reveals that the Jew and Gentile are two children who are equally loved" Are you not as the children of Ethiopia to me, children of Israel?" (Amos 9:7.)

Second, a branch thought of election emerges here, one that states that all nations are fundamentally alike in the eyes of God because God is still the Creator of man. Yet, God has selected Israel, which can be seen from the prophet Amos, "You only have I known of all the families of the earth; therefore, I will punish you for all your iniquities."

From the words if Amos, Israel was to understand that their divine selection is owed not to ethnic or national superiority. Neither does their election release them from punishment for their sins. Still, Jewish election is reinforced by the idea of divine providence (Amos 3:2 KJV.)

◆◆◆

When God chose to reveal Himself to a specific small group, it was simply divine providence. This choosing of Israel was not because they were more numerous. They were, in fact, the smallest and weakest of nations (Deuteronomy 7:7.) It was not for power and material well-being, as well. It was for righteous and ethical purposes. It was even for the benefit of all nations.

Articulating these principles leads us yet to another branch thought and concept of Israel's election. That is, when the nations fall into the depths of idolatry and materialism, God will raise up one small group to establish the ideal of the One True God again. This is an enduring call for any remnant that rises up in history; it is the definition of the remnant call!

Still, no nation can take Israel's place historically or biblically. This brings us to the relationship between election to be chosen.

DEFINING JEWISH ELECTION

To grasp the idea of the Jewish election further, we turn to Romans 11:29. No one speaks of the election as the Apostle Paul, "God's gifts and His call are irrevocable." But how Dispensational and Reformed theologians see the relationship

111

between Israel and the church is different.

Historically, dispensationalists believe that God has two separate programs in history, one for Israel and one for the church and that the two groups are totally unrelated. Reformed theologians believe that the promises made to Israel, have been, or will be, fulfilled in the church and that God no longer has a special relationship with the nation of Israel. But Romans teaches, "that God has not rejected His people, and so all Israel will be saved, as it is written" (Romans 11:26.) "All Israel" is subject to interpretation by many.

John Calvin believed that "All Israel" pertained to all the redeemed, both Jews and gentiles. If correct, Paul is expressing the idea that when the full number of people is saved, then all Israel will be saved, because the two are synonymous. This view ignores the fact that Paul speaks of Israel and the gentiles as two distinct groups. Here the Jewish people experienced a hardening until the full number of gentiles has been saved, and Israel will then turn from their unbelief and be saved.

Despite everything, Paul in verses 1-32, claims that while Israel's unbelief is purposeful, it is temporary. Always he is leaning towards partial hardening, not the Historical-Christian view towards complete and permanent rejection. As one reads verses 33-36, one immediately sees Paul's understanding of God's wisdom and knowledge throughout the entire passage.

Stating it again, the church has assumed that a full hardening has taken place with little or no chance of a return for the Jew. Therefore, they have become the new heirs. In the following Chapter, we bring to light more pieces of this puzzle and explore further, the Jewish people and the Messianic Kingdom to come. But it is important to simply see "election "as conveying the same idea of "chosen-ness." When it comes to the New Testament, the Greek word ekloge means divine selection or chosen. In the Old Testament, the Hebrew word bachiyr means chosen, chosen one, or the elect of God.

The question that remains is, what was Israel and the Jewish people are historically chosen for? This is first answered in Exodus 19:5-6 (KJV): "Now, therefore, if ye will obey My word and keep My covenant, then ye shall be a peculiar treasure unto Me above all people, for all the earth is Mine. And ye shall be unto Me a kingdom of priests and a holy nation."

Isaiah writes in chapter 42:6, "I will keep you and will make you be a covenant for the people and a light for the gentiles." This meant they were given the mission to make people recognize the Almighty's sovereignty and to help them believe in Him. Below is their complete calling as memorialized in Scripture:

♦♦♦

[1] REVEAL THE ONE TRUE GOD TO THE NATIONS: Exodus 19:5-6. "if you obey me fully and keep my covenant, then out of all nations, you will be my treasured possession. Although the whole earth is mine, you will be for me a kingdom of priests and a holy nation.' These are the words you are to speak to the Israelites." NIV

[2] BENEFICIARY OF GOD'S REVELATION: Deuteronomy 4:5-9; Romans 3:1-2. "see, I have taught you decrees and laws as the LORD my God commanded me, so that you may follow them in the land you are entering to take possession of it. [6] Observe them carefully, for this will show your wisdom and understanding to the nations, who will hear about all these decrees and say, "Surely this great nation is a wise and understanding people." [7] What other nation is so great as to have their God's near them the way the LORD our God is near us whenever we pray to him? 8 And what other nation is so great as to have such righteous decrees and laws as this body of laws I am setting before you today? (Deuteronomy 4:5-8 NIV.)."What advantage, then, is there in being a Jew, or what value is there in circumcision? Much in every way! First of all, they have been entrusted with the very words of God (Romans 3:1-2 NIV).

[3] PROLIFERATE THE DOCTRINE OF THE ONE TRUE GOD: Isaiah 43; 11-12 You are my witnesses," declares the LORD, "and my servant whom I have chosen, so that you may know and believe me and understand that I am he. Before me no god was formed, nor will there be one after me. 11 I, even I, am the LORD, and apart from me, there is no savior. 12 I have revealed and saved and proclaimed — I, and not some foreign god among you."

[4] HEAD OF THE NATIONS: Deuteronomy 28:12-13. "The LORD will open the heavens, the storehouse of his bounty, to send rain on your land in season and to bless all the work of your hands. You will lend to many nations but will borrow from none. 13 The LORD will make you the head, not the tail. If you pay attention to the commands of the LORD your God that I give you this day and carefully follow them, you will always be at the top, never at the bottom. "NIV.

[5]CARETAKERS and DEFENDERS OF GOD'S VINEYARD, ISRAEL: The famous thirteenth-century exegete and Biblical scholar Moses Nachmanides, interprets the phrase," for the land is mine" in Leviticus 25:23, "Here God is speaking to Israel through Moses; "You are but stranger's residents with me." From two other translations, "The land must not be sold permanently, because the land is mine and you are but aliens and my tenants." (TNIV.) "And remember, the land is mine, so you may not sell it permanently. You are merely My tenants and sharecroppers" (NLT.) In conclusion, no one can own the Holy Land with any permanency other than God.

END OF CHAPTER QUESTIONS

1. In 70 AD the Roman army led by Titus destroyed the Temple and sacked Jerusalem, the spiritual center of Judaism at the time.

2. In what way was the Acts 15 Jerusalem Council reflecting the new Jewish leadership in this early period.

3. Following the resurrection of our Messiah they gathered on the first day of the week, which was called the Lord's Day. This evolved into the Christian Sabbath of which the Catholic Church seems to have taken claim. What is the difference between the Lord's Day, and the Sabbath, which is found in the 4th commandment of the Torah. Which one should be observed?

4. Explain the foolishness of the historical charge of blaming the Jewish people for killing Jesus? What impact did it have on Judaism as well as the Church?

5. Describe Replacement Theology, Dispensationalism, and its impact on the mission of the Church to reach the Jew.

6. What is Jewish election, and where can it be supported in the Scripture?

7. What are five areas of calling upon the Jewish people?

CHAPTER SIX

Israel and the Messianic Kingdom

SINCE LITTLE SYSTEMATIC TEACHING IS GIVEN ON THIS TOPIC OF THE MESSIANIC KINGDOM, and prophecy is in high gear today, it is vital to know the future Messianic Kingdom as it relates to the Jewish people and Israel. Christian culture can foster a culture of escapism, as many believers view heaven as our final destination. Though heaven is eternal, and is one of our destinations, God's ultimate fulfillment is the restoration of the earth. So, the earth is not a provisional fuel rocket that we jettison to merely reach our permanent home in heaven.

Further, Israel holds a centerpiece position in the restoration to come, and we will explore the government in this future Kingdom in order to capture the fullness of Israel's role in God's plan. But for now, it is important to rethink eternity and the dimension of life that awaits us.

WHAT IS ETERNITY?

Another piece of understanding that needs a new light shed upon it is the fact, that many have understood eternity as that time when we enter our heavenly homes/mansions that Yeshua promised His followers in John 14:2-4 states, "In my Father's house are many mansions: if it were not so, I would have told you. I go to prepare a place for you. In addition, if I go and prepare a place for you, I will come again and receive you unto myself; that where I am, there thee may also be".

Eternity, is not a particular location. Rather, eternity is a dimension of living t when one is liberated from this corruptible state and body. Only then do we enter the incorruptible state of being. Putting it in these terms.

Eternity is when a man passes beyond the finite and is no longer dependent upon this material realm. During this time, heaven is one of our destinations, but it is only temporary. Our final destination is the earth in all of its pre-prescribed glory and wholeness that our Creator initially intended. There God's entire plan is predesigned to operate in the eternal realm for all the earth to be righteously governed.

> "God laid the foundations of the earth, "that it should not be removed forever." Then 24:7-10, "Lift up your heads, O ye gates; and be ye lift up ye everlasting doors, and the King of glory shall come in.8 who is this King of glory? The LORD who strong and mighty, the LORD mighty in battle.9 Lift up your heads, O ye gates; even lift them up, ye everlasting doors; and the King of glory shall come in.10, who is this King of glory? The LORD of hosts, he is the King of glory."
>
> (Psalm 104:5.)

THE MESSIANIC KINGDOM

The importance of this study revolves around the fact that most misunderstand the future age as purely spiritual and ethereal. And while many presume there is no distinction between the Jew and gentile, and Israel and the nations, this traditional idea is untrue to the facts. Specifically, the future Messianic Kingdom is God's final antidote to the poisonous teaching of replacement theology, anti-Semitism, and all of humanity's flaws. This new order will be rigorously righteous, and Israel will come into her full, irrevocable calling.

Second, what was once the garden era, the most ideal time mankind has ever known, every sphere of life will be transformed and pointed towards God's original design in the Messianic Kingdom. Only then will man finally grasp his rightful place in this universe. During this time, all competition between man and man will be of a past age. Competition and territorialism in the Church will be gone. Those long turned off to religion will, at last, find religious solidarity; one faith, one Messiah, and one religious system will exist where every nation and tongue will worship the Lord God of Abraham, Isaac, and Jacob.

For those who have suffered much due to loss and grief, mourning will give way to joy, as death will give way to life, and war will give way to peace. The human government will finally yield to the righteous rule of the Messianic kingdom, and Jerusalem will be its capital city. When it comes to nature, it will be wonderfully transformed. Mothers will no longer experience a miscarriage or children die prematurely; sickness and disease, along with infant mortality, will be of the past. Political, genocide and ethnic cleansing will be of a past age. Even the animal kingdom, with its predatory spirit, will be removed as the lion will lie down with the lamb and eat straw like the ox.

Something that has never occurred, peace will finally be at Israel's borders as God returns all the Jewish people to their "full and restored" Promised Land. 2 (End of the book) I believe God will also return the nations back to their God-given geographic boundaries.

The whole point of revival in the future age is to allow a man to take hold of the fuller meaning of God's purpose. In this, the nations will finally see their own life in relation to His sovereign plan for the earth, and their connection to Israel. Isaiah the prophet sees a universal kingdom in terms of Zion and Jerusalem like no other prophet: "For out of Zion shall go forth the law and the word of the Lord from Jerusalem"
(Isaiah 2: 3 NKJV.)

Even the Psalms focus upon this religious and historical attitude toward Jerusalem: "If I forget thee, O Jerusalem, let my right hand forget her cunning. If I do not remember thee, let my tongue cleave to the roof of my mouth; if I prefer not Jerusalem above my chief joy" (Psalm 137:5-6 KJV.)

THE KINGDOM OF HEAVEN /
THE KINGDOM OF GOD

When we think of the kingdom of Heaven, the one that creation groans for, and the one that we pray for in the Lord's Prayer

(Matthew 6:10,) I think of government. However, the kingdom of heaven also refers to the origin of this Kingdom. It speaks of the place from which the Kingdom is coming. It is not the destination that we are going to.

The kingdom of Heaven then is a kingdom from heaven, not a kingdom in heaven. When it arrives, it will pull all things back towards God's original plan. This understanding is significant to end-time understanding. In this future time, Yeshua will return as King over the earth. He comes to administer the distinction between the kingdom of heaven and the kingdom of God. This provides the foundation to see God's plan for a future government that is inclusive of Israel and the Jewish people. And for this reason alone, Israel will never be removed from the earth.

IT'S POLITY: GOVERNMENT

In this future kingdom on earth, a political kingdom whose polity will be of the Ancient of Days will be established. Nothing less than the quintessential Monarchy whose Head will be Yeshua, where He will rule the entire earth. The prophet Daniel pinpoints this far into the future of himself when he writes, "the wind swept them away without leaving a trace. But the rock that struck the statue became a huge mountain and filled the earth" (Daniel 2:45.)

What should be clear is that the kingdom of Heaven is inseparable from the kingdom of God. This is because all matters and dimensions of life, both here, and into the spiritual realms, is part of the kingdom of God. In other words, life, grand or small, political or spiritual, regional, international, universal or beyond, operate in the kingdom of God. This is because God is unlimited and sovereign over all creation. This includes the planetary and solar systems (Revelation 4:11.)

In Psalm 139, the same sentiment is expressed, "Such knowledge is too wonderful for me, too lofty for me to attain. Where can I go from your Spirit? Where can I flee from your presence? If I go up to the heavens, you are there; if I make my bed in the depths, you are there...." In the kingdom of Heaven, however, Yeshua will be sovereign over the earth, and His seat of power will be in Jerusalem.

Hence, the kingdom of Heaven lasts for one thousand years, while the kingdom of God has no beginning and no end, and it is timeless and limitless. This kingdom of heaven will be Hebraic in order, earthly in location, and material and spiritual in substance, while the kingdom of God is angelic, heavenly, and mostly invisible.

As we look far into the future, a time will come when the magnificent kingdom of God and the kingdom Heaven will be as two interlocking spheres. They will be like wheels turning within wheels. Revelation 11:15 states, "the kingdom of the world has become the kingdom of our Lord and of his Christ; and he will reign forever and ever" NIV. Another passage that conveys the same idea,

"And I saw a new heaven and a new earth: for the first heaven and the first earth were passed away; and there was no more sea. 2 And I John saw the holy city, New

Jerusalem, coming down from God out of heaven, prepared as a bride adorned for her husband."

(Revelation 21:1-2.)

JEWS and the KINGDOM

When it comes to the Jewish people, and the kingdom, the teaching of the Messianic Kingdom has always represented a future hope. The saying: t'hiyat ha-metim, means the revival of the body. In these words, is an anticipation of a resurrection in the life to come. This is illustrated in the Amidah prayer that is recited by observant Jews daily: "Thou art forever almighty, Lord, bringing alive the dead...in Thine abundant compassion...Thou keepest faith with those who sleep in the dust...Thou art dependable to revive the dead."

Jewish prayers point to this long-standing hope when they anticipate a better future after the dead are raised to new life. God giving Israel the Torah of truth, He planted everlasting life in their midst, "all Israel will share in the world to come" (Sanhedrin 10:1.) 3" Also, the term, "Olam ha-ba," means "a share in the world to come." The following three ideas come to light:

♦♦♦

[1] The soul comes from God and must return to Him is established in Judaism.

[2] God intended for the world to be as the Garden of Eden, which sin destroyed — The coming of Messiah is the coming full circle of that ideal.

[3] The Resurrection of the Dead: The Sabbath prayer states, "This prayer brings forth this ideal: There is no comparison to You HaShem in this world, and there will be nothing except for You, our King, in the life of the world to come; there will be nothing without You, our Redeemer, in the Messianic days; and there will be none as You, our Savior and resurrection of the dead."

For the Jew then, the mark of God's rule was always Israel living in their fullness. For the Christian church, their focus has long remained the cross, the resurrection, and the ascension. The Jew sees Jerusalem and Mt. Zion restored. The Christian sees the "New Jerusalem" coming down out of heaven, as seen in Revelation 21:2.

Also, there is a fulfillment that comes when the full working power of God, takes place through the blood of Yeshua. Yet, a future spiritual form of its own is awaiting us. This is called the incorruptible state. When the Kingdom arrives upon the earth as noted earlier, a material government will take hold where both the Jew and Gentile will serve together in. The incorruptible that have been raptured will co-reign with Messiah. Read I Corinthians 15:53, and Revelation 5:10).

PART II

Kingdom Government

Beginning from the Government of Messiah's Kingdom on earth, the world will, at last, witness God's plan of which Israel completes. The plan though, is not just for one people, but the whole human race. Still, the Jewish people move up to universal headship for the first time, perhaps since the Davidic Dynasty, The Golden Era, and the Monarchy of Solomon.

When King David, Solomon, the Old Testament Prophets, the Twelve Tribes of Israel, the Jewish Apostles, and the great men of God listed in the hall of fame of faith in Hebrews chapter 12 were laid to rest in the tombs of their fathers, their election did not die with them.

Counter to popular belief, they will rise in the resurrection with a distinction remaining between Jew and Gentile. But both Jew and Gentile will advance to their God-given destiny. One thing is sure, the Government rests at the center of God's sphere of administration. This is true in Heaven, on earth, and in the Kingdom to come. In fact, this principle of Government is the vista upon which we can look out and discover the election of Israel, and this remains one of the central purposes of the Messianic Age.

Isaiah spoke of the Jewish-Messianic vision in terms of Zion and Jerusalem. Namely, that out of Zion shall go forth the Torah with the Word of God from Jerusalem (Isaiah 2:3.)

Similar passages are seen in Psalms focusing upon this attitude toward Jerusalem, "If I forget thee, O Jerusalem, let my right hand forget her cunning. Let my tongue cleave to the roof of my mouth, if I remember thee not; if I set not Jerusalem above my chiefest joy" (Psalm 137:5-6.) These hopes infused Israel with faith, and a longing for the Kingdom of Heaven to fulfill God's plan for planet earth.

THY KINGDOM COME

When we study the Gospel accounts of Matthew, Mark, Luke, and John, including the opening chapters of the book of Acts, we notice a leading subject on the kingdom of heaven. With all of God's glory, this kingdom will descend from heaven to earth, and Israel will finally acquire their set role as the Chosen People.

Finally, they will move into their elected offices, and the Messianic kingdom will display God's purpose for planet earth. This will take place in every sphere, governmentally, geographically, politically, spiritually, and socially.

The Gentile will also be serving side by side with the Jewish people in complete and final harmony. In this future government, there will be no favoritism due to one's lineage, or family connections praise God. Justice will be swift and perfect because the one ruling will be the Lion of Judah from His Holy Mountain (Psalms 149: 6-9; Corinthians. 6:2; Revelation 5:10; 20:4-6.)

Since Heaven does not operate randomly, and as noted, through a discernable chain of command (government.) Spirit beings are always operating for our Creator's will. They are not independent or self-seeking as man, but they also have rank and responsibility.

Consider the Cherubim in Genesis 3:24 and Exodus 5:18-20, or the Seraphim in Isaiah 6: 2-3, and Gabriel and Michael the Archangel who is known as the defender of Israel (Luke 1:19, 26; Daniel 8:16; 9:20-23; Revelation 12:7; Jude 9:9; Daniel 10:13-14,) These are all governmental offices. And with tens of thousands of legions of these spiritual agencies, called also ministering angels, the redeemed of the Lord are ministered too daily by an army of these angelic beings(Hebrews 1:14.)

♦♦♦

I am reminded of when Yeshua ascended to heaven and the words that were spoken in 1 Peter 3:22; "He who has gone into heaven and is at God's right hand — with angels, authorities, and powers in submission to him." Yet, in this future government, a tangible and material rule will exist. In his book "The Footsteps of Messiah," Dr. Arnold Fruchtenbaum refers to a [Gentile] branch and a [Jewish] branch of government. Any governmental distinction is an administrative one, and not a sign of greater endearment over another as many have thought.

When we turn to the Scriptures, we discover the former king David who returns to reign under King Yeshua as prince over earthly Israel. He will not be the Crowned Head, because Yeshua will sit upon the throne as the ultimate Monarch King. However, the Scripture provides for various rulers as these, which are called priests, and princes, particularly when it comes to David. Take a moment to reflect on this Davidic order to come. It is the source of the Lord's Prayer, "thy kingdom come."

A FUTURE DAVIDIC ORDER

With a flawless Davidic order moving into place, it will, of course, involve the former King David, or prince David, "Afterward the Israelites will return and seek the LORD their God and David, their king. They will come trembling to the LORD and to his blessings in the last day" (Hosea 3:5.) The prophet Jeremiah reveals the same, "But they shall serve the LORD their God, and David their king, whom I will raise up unto them" (Jeremiah 39:9 KJV.)

Other Jewish prophets envisioned a time when David will return, "I will place over them one shepherd, my servant David, and he will tend them; he will tend them and be their shepherd. I the LORD will be their God, and my servant David will be prince among them" (Ezekiel 34:23.) Consider the following governmental offices in the future kingdom of the Messiah that will comprise the order of the age to come.

THE TWELVE JEWISH APOSTLES

Matthew and Luke provide information regarding the twelve Apostles who will literally rule over the nation of Israel after Israel's national regeneration. Jesus said to them, "I tell you the truth, at the renewal of all things, when the Son of Man sits on his glorious throne, you who have followed me will also sit on twelve thrones, judging the twelve tribes of Israel" (Matthew 19:28-29.) Also, "you are those who have stood by me in my trials. And I confer on you a kingdom, just as my Father conferred one on me, so that you may eat and drink at my table in my kingdom and sit on thrones, judging the twelve tribes of Israel," (Luke 22:27-30.)

ABRAHAM, ISAAC, and JACOB

In Matthew 8:11 it states, "And I say unto you, that many shall come from the east and west and shall sit down with Abraham, and Isaac, and Jacob, in the kingdom of heaven." Abraham, Isaac, and Jacob will also be resurrected in the Messianic kingdom, and" many will come from the east and the west, to sit down with them.

RIGHTEOUS JUDGES and COUNSELORS

What has never taken place before, the slighted scales of justice that has always served the wealthy will be no more; "Behold, a king shall reign in righteousness, and princes shall rule in judgment" (Isaiah 32:1). From Ezekiel," in the land shall be his possession in Israel: and my princes shall no more oppress my people, and the rest of the land shall they give to the house of Israel according to their tribes" (Ezekiel 45:8). Isaiah carries this" same theme regarding judges and counselors; "I will restore your judges as in days of old, your counselors as at the beginning. Afterward, you will be called the City of Righteousness, the Faithful City" (Isaiah 1:26.)

The offices mentioned above repeatedly shows that the first law of Heaven is order. And the government carries out everything God desires. One of Messiah's final acts was to install the" ascension gifts that order is created in the" body while in His" absence. Take a moment to review the following,

> "Now that he ascended, what is it but that he also descended first into the lower parts of the earth? He that descended is the same also that ascended far above all heavens, that he might fill all things.) 11 And he gave some, apostles; and some, prophets; and some, evangelists; and some, pastors and teachers; 12 For the perfecting of the saints, for the work of the ministry, for the edifying of the body of Christ: 13 Till we all come in the unity of the faith, and of the knowledge of the Son of God, unto a perfect man, unto the measure of the stature of the fullness of Christ, 14 That we henceforth be no more children, tossed to and fro, and carried about with every wind of doctrine, by the sleight of men, and cunning craftiness, whereby they lie in wait to deceive"
>
> (Ephesians 4:9-14.)

Again, the order is seen in Peter's actions to replace Judas one of the twelve. Why could they not proceed with the eleven? Because a certain order and structure was needed (Acts 1:25-26.) Matthew and Luke inform us that the twelve apostles will literally rule over the twelve tribes of Israel after Israel's national regeneration; this again is a governmental formula. Twelve being a governmental number, along with the twelve tribes, there are twelve pillars (Exodus 24:4) and twelve men chosen by Joshua (Joshua 4:4.)

> "I tell you the truth, at the renewal of all things, when the Son of Man sits on his glorious throne, you who have followed me will also sit on twelve thrones, judging the twelve tribes of Israel."
>
> (Matthew 19:28-29.)

> "You are those who have stood by me in my trials. And I confer on you a kingdom, just as my Father conferred one on me, so that you may eat and drink at my table in my kingdom and sit on thrones, judging the twelve tribes of Israel."
>
> (Luke 22:27-30.)

It should also be noted, when believers rebel against spiritual, biblical offices, they rebel not against man, but against God's governmental order. Consequently, the body of the Messiah can use a new revelation of this in the end times that we find ourselves in today.

THE END of DAYS RESURRECTION

A central principle of both Judaism and Christianity is the resurrection of the dead. The Talmud states, "If the womb, which receives in silence, yet brings forth amid great cries of jubilation, then the grave, which receives the dead amid cries of grief, will much more so bring them forth amid great cries of joy" (Sanhedrin 92a.)

Resurrections were often associated with great moments in the advancement of the kingdom on earth. This will be no different in the future. In Yeshua's day, a mighty resurrection occurred, the tombs broke open, and the bodies of many holy people who had died were raised to life" (Matthew 27:52.) As Abraham, Isaac, and Jacob (the Biblical forefathers) are resurrected, every nation will have the opportunity to sit down with them in Jerusalem. For sure, we will all be worshipping together at the Feast of Tabernacles, "And I say unto you, that many shall come from the east and" west and shall sit down with Abraham, and Isaac, and Jacob, in the kingdom of heaven" (Zechariah 14:6 NIV.)

When it comes to the former King David, we have noted earlier, and he will be resurrected with all the other Old Testament great men and women of faith that have long gone before us—prophets and prophetesses. All will return to fulfill God's order and government in the kingdom to come, and, within their God-given identity and calling. The Prophet Daniel speaks of a resurrection in chapter 11 and 12, with his last three verses dealing with the redemption of Israel:

> "And many of them that sleep in the dust of the earth shall awake, some to everlasting life, and some to reproaches and everlasting abhorrence" (12:2.) Daniel does not say all of them, and he states many of them that sleep, (the righteous, who have fallen asleep in the former age,) will return to usher in a Davidic order upon the earth. The Prophet provides a fascinating look into his future: "Go thy way, Daniel: for the words are closed up and sealed till the time of the end. Many shall be purified, and made white, and tried, but the wicked shall do wickedly: and none of the wicked shall understand, but the wise shall understand. And from the time that the daily sacrifice shall be taken away, and the abomination that maketh desolate setup, there shall be a thousand two hundred and ninety days. Blessed is he that waiteth, and cometh to the thousand three hundred and five and thirty days. But go thou thy way till the end be: for thou shalt rest, and stand in thy lot at the end of the days."
>
> (Daniel 12: 9-13 KJV.)

It appears that after the three and a half years of the tribulation, there will be an additional 45 days, totaling 1,335 days, counting from the abomination in the temple. This added period of future blessing assures Daniel and all the Old Testament saints a vital part in the Davidic kingdom when here they will apparently be resurrected.

CONCLUSION

The kingdom is what all creation has been groaning for. I personally groan for God's order to come to earth more than ever. In looking forward to that time, the Jewish people will arise and "Call Him Blessed," realize who their God and King is, and finally step into her elected offices. The entire earth will finally witness the completion of Israel's irrevocable calling…how good and pleasant it will be for both Jew and Gentile — hineh ma Tov u-mah na'im, achim.

As a final note, if there are some gentiles that feel excluded due to so much attention upon Israel and the Jewish people in the Kingdom to come, consider these words of Isaiah who gives us a beautiful portrayal of the future temple ministry that awaits them,

> "Also the sons of the stranger, that join themselves to the LORD, to serve Him, and to love the name of the LORD, to be his servants, everyone that keep the Sabbath from polluting it, and take hold of my covenant; Even them will I bring to my holy mountain, and make them joyful in my house of prayer: their burnt offerings and their sacrifices shall be accepted upon mine altar; for mine, house shall be called a house of prayer for all people. [8]The Lord GOD, which gathers the outcasts of Israel saith, yet will I gather others to him, beside those that are gathered unto him. (Isaiah 56:10-8)

END CHAPTER QUESTIONS

1. Describe Eternity and its characteristics of this future habitation.

2. Can you explain the difference between the Kingdom of God and the Kingdom of Heaven?

3. What relevance does the understanding of the Kingdom of Heaven have to the Jewish people and Israel?

4. Explain aspects of the Messianic Kingdom/ government upon Messiah's Second coming.

5. What is Israel's role in the Messianic Kingdom? How does this relate to the Irrevocable call in Romans 11:29?

6. What is the end of days resurrection, and show from Scripture the return of the former King David and the Patriarchs?

CHAPTER SEVEN

The Jewish Root Severed

DURING THE APOSTOLIC PERIOD, AD 1-100, AND THE ANTE-NICENE PERIOD, AD 100-325, a collision course between Judaism and the political machine of Rome was in motion. With a vast growing body of Hellenistic believers beginning to enroll themselves in a new state religion called Christianity, these new adherents came through Constantine's Christianity, and with their hearts and minds permeated by Plato and Greek worldview. The context of the day was a Greek-Roman world.

When Rome rose to power with a mighty military and a highly developed government, Greek culture still dominated something far more captivating—the mind. It permeated philosophy, art, science, and architecture. Greek became the language of culture. It was common for Jews to have a Greek name and, of course, a Hebrew name, which was particularly important in areas like Jerusalem. Communicating in both Greek and Hebrew was important.

For the Lord Himself, He was known as Yeshua to the Jewish community and Jesus to the Hellenists. The mother of Yeshua, Mary, was known as Miriam to her Jewish family and friends. Paul was known as Saul in Hebrew, and Paul to the Greeks after God changed His name. But how Jewish identity in Messiah evolved, and how it influenced church culture and Hellenistic thinking, is an important issue.

Fundamentally, when Yeshua came two thousand years ago, He tied together for all time the Old and the New Testament forming one binding testimony. Essentially, he tied together Judaism with her missing part to complete her. This enabled Jews and gentiles to see a new path that accommodated both while forming one compact unit and body.

But history would be shaped inversely. What I mean to say is. This unity of One New Man, Jew, and Gentile, would come later. It is being understood only in our time. Still, one can look at many scriptures, and see the Jewish context and culture of two thousand years ago, and discover, sparkling truths that are rich in Jewish culture and context. Mostly, one realizes how inseparable Jew and Gentile are, and how their destinies are inexplicably linked.

THE JEWISH MESSIAH

In the eyes of many of His day, Yeshua was, in fact, the authentic Maschiach. Many accepted Him as the fulfillment of the Old Testament Prophets. Belief in Yeshua then is one that is two thousand years old. It began not with marginal or cultural Jews, but Orthodox Jews. And though He was seen as a Jewish scholar and prophet, He had a message that was radical to the religious establishment that mystified the greatest scholars of His day.

His miracles captured the attention of the multitudes

because they were miracles that only the Messiah could carry out. Like delivering the deaf and dumb demoniac in Matthew chapter 12. Yeshua was born of a Jewish mother and father, circumcised on the eighth day, and was brought up to fulfill the commandments of the Torah. As a Jew, Yeshua likely recited the ancient Psalms, the 18 Benedictions, also the Avino Malkenu (Our Father Our King.)

Yeshua came from the tribe of Judah of the line of David, and from a priestly clan of the highest order that predated even the Aaronic and Levitical priesthood, the line of Melchizedek, (Genesis 14:18; Psalms 110:1,4; Zechariah 6:13; Hebrews 5:1,4,5, 7; 6:19; 7:1.) Yet, throughout Church history and in our present day, Yeshua has been presented to the Jewish people with a prerequisite of forsaking their Jewish cultural heritage.

Imagine Paul this former Pharisee (Acts 22:3-4) standing in the synagogue in Pisidian Antioch giving testimony that God brought Israel the Messiah, the one from the line of David (Acts 13:23.) Or Timothy, one who was schooled in the Torah from a child to prepare him for salvation later when the Jewish Messiah would come (2 Timothy 3:15.) And finally, Peter, a former Pharisee, who lived a life according to the strict dietary laws of Judaism (Acts 11:4-9.)

♦♦♦

Regarding Yeshua and all Orthodox Jewish males, Numbers 15:38-41 and Deuteronomy 22:12 required them to wear fringes on their garments called tzitzit, which represented the commandments. In Matthew 9:21, a woman presses through the crowd in order to touch these fringes. But on this day, she was touching the living commandments because the Word had become flesh.

Consider Revelation 22:18-19 with its strong warning against altering the Word of God compared with the same Teaching in the Jewish Talmud in Sanhedrin 90, "If one prophesies as to eradicate a law from the Torah he is liable to death." Finally, when it comes to Yeshua's end-time warnings that are given in 2 Timothy 3:19 and Matthew 10:35, the Talmud has similar signs,

> "In the footsteps of the Messiah insolence will increase, youths will put old men to shame, the old will stand up in the presence of the young, a son will revile his father, a daughter will rise against her mother, a daughter in law against her mother in law and a man's enemies will be the members of his household. The face of the generation will be like the face of a dog (impervious to shame.) A son will not feel ashamed before his father, so upon whom is it for us to rely upon? Upon our father, who is in heaven, man will become more and more debased," (Sotah 49b).

A religious leader confronted Yeshua and asked Him, what is the greatest commandment in the Law, He said, Yeshua and asked Him, what is the greatest commandment in the Law He said,

> "Love the Lord your God with all your heart and with all your soul and with all your mind. This is the first and greatest commandment. And the second is like it:

'Love your neighbor as yourself. All the Law and the Prophets hang on these two commandments." (Matthew 22:35-40.)

When asked to sum up Judaism in few moments, Hillel the great Palestinian sage echoed the same, "That which is hurtful to thee, do not do to thy neighbor, this is the whole doctrine, the rest is commentary, now go forth and learn." The term "neighbor" in Matthew refers to fellow Israelites, countrymen. We often miss this meaning of the term neighbor in the context of Jewish understanding. In Exodus 20:16, it speaks about "bearing false witness against thy neighbor," it meant your fellow Israelite, brother, companion, husband, even lover. It refers to those that you are in a relationship with, and are equally yoked with.

In other words, Scripture provides specific instructions on how fellow brothers and sisters in the Lord are to treat one another, even for us today. In Ephesians 4:25, "Therefore, each of you must put off falsehood and speak truthfully, to his "neighbor," For we are all members of one body". The essential truth here is that one cannot love one another if one does not love themselves first, and the body of the Messiah cannot love the world if it has not learned to love one another.

As the Jewish religious establishment said no to Yeshua, Jews that believe in Yeshua today are left with a historical paradox. According to the traditional Jewish view, a Jew cannot be Jewish if one believes in the Jewish Messiah. Yet, Jews can adhere to Buddhism, Hinduism, Taoism, New Age philosophy,

Agnosticism, or even Atheism, and still be considered Jewish. More, Jews can discard Jewish beliefs and practices yet remain Jewish in the eyes of the Jewish community. But Jews who embrace thoroughly Jewish beliefs in the Jewish Messiah and live thoroughly Jewish lives, are not regarded as Jews.

Out of the five major sects of Judaism today (Reformed, Conservative, Orthodox, Re-constructionist, and Humanistic), the last two are the most conflicting when making anti-Jewish claims of Jewish believers in Yeshua. Consider their brief descriptions below.

♦♦♦

- Re-constructionist Judaism: An evolving religious civilization, but does not believe that God chose the Jewish people. It does believe in a personified deity that is active in history. Most do not believe that God can reveal Himself to man, and therefore, reject the belief that God personally chose the Jewish people.
- Humanistic Judaism: A non-theistic belief (no belief in God.) Established in 1963 in Detroit, Michigan by Rabbi Sherwin T. Wine, it offers a non-theistic alternative to current Jewish life. Humanistic Jews believe in a meaningful Jewish lifestyle that is free from supernatural authority; it is a human-centered philosophy combined with the celebration of Jewish culture and identity with humanistic values.

In spite of what we have cited, let's return to our discussion on the Institutional Church. As the early Church needed a new living organism or Christian expression apart from Judaism, the Jewish root would be cut from the foundations of the New Covenant faith; this would include the Jewish people. The simple question is how did it happen?

♦♦♦

We have noted the destruction of the temple early on, and attributing it to God's rejection of His people and holding the Jewish people responsible for Christ's death. These few notables in church history alone, fostered anti-Jewish paradigms, and heart attitudes that created bias views against Jews. Then they were perpetuated from generation-to-generation, germinated from seminary-to-seminary, and from denomination-to-denomination. Their potency upon church history was powerful enough to survive today.

Therefore, as one studies early Church history, you discover that the relationship between the Jewish world and the early New Covenant Roman world was one of hostility and deep social pressure on the Jews. Consider the following words of Cicero, a Roman orator, politician, and philosopher, who spoke of the Roman world and the Jews before the destruction of the second temple:

> "Even while Jerusalem was still standing the Jews were at peace with us, the practice of their sacred rites, however, were at variance with the glory of our empire, the dignity of our name, the customs of our ancestors" [3]
>
> Cicero (106-43 BCE.)

As empire life (the Roman Christian world) became difficult on Jews, Jews that wanted to embrace Yeshua either for real reasons or political and economic had to renounce their Jewish identity and turn from the faith of their Biblical forefathers. Jews were forced to convert to a gentile form of faith. In his book Restoring the Jewishness of the Gospel, David Stern notes that the Jews were required to swear to and sign the following:

> "I renounce all customs, rites, legalisms, unleavened breads and sacrifices of lambs of the Hebrews, and all the other Feasts of the Hebrews, sacrifices, prayers, aspersions, purifications, sanctifications, and propitiations, and fasts, and new moons, and Sabbaths, and superstitions, and hymns and chants and observances and synagogues, and the food and drink of the Hebrews. In a word, I renounce absolutely everything Jewish, every law, rite, and custom—and if afterward I shall wish to deny and return to Jewish superstitions, or shall be found eating with Jews, or feasting with them, or secretly conversing and condemning the Christian religion instead of openly confuting them and condemning their vain faith, then let the trembling of Cain and the leprosy of Gehazi cleave to me, as well as the legal punishments to which I acknowledge myself liable. And may I be an anathema in the world to come, and my soul be set down with Satan and the devils' (End of book references)

In 306 AD, at the Synod of Elvira in 306 AD, 5 Jews were prohibited from marrying Christians, forbidden to have sexual intercourse together. Rulings during that same period prohibited Jews and Christians from eating together. Later in 535AD at the Synod of Clermont, Jews were forbidden to hold public office, and at the 3rd Synod of Orleans in 538 AD, Jews could not walk on public streets during Christian Passion week.

◆ ◆ ◆

- In 335 AD, Constantine decreed that any slave circumcised by a Jewish master was freed. Soon after (337 AD), laws were created that banned any Jew from bothering, harassing, or causing damage to Jews who converted to Christianity.

- At the Synod of Szabolcs (1902), it became illegal for Jews to work on Sunday, the Christian Sabbath. Jews were forbidden to be plaintiffs or witnesses against Christians in the court…the law became stacked against the Jew. What is inconceivable, Jews were prohibited from living in Jerusalem or passing through the city.

Consequently, as the Jew became viewed as the rejected people of God, a people who had lost their covenantal inheritance, the Church saw themselves as their replacement, the new chosen people. And as Judaism evolved into this rejected religion, the Torah was misinterpreted in the areas dealing with Israel and the Jewish people, which pre-disposed subsequent generations to be unaware of anything Jewish. Hence, the Christian Church environment became anti-Semitic or anti-Jewish. Below are a personal testimony and encounter with this historical difficulty with the Jewish people and the Church only 40 years ago.

PERSONAL TESTIMONY WITH ANTI-SEMITISM

Only forty-two years ago, my wife and I were preparing to get married when we were confronted with this historical issue. Raised with deep Jewish values, my Wife's faith in Yeshua was still fresh and taking root. As we began searching for guidance from one of the local ministers, he cited the following stipulations for my wife; deny your Jewish family, renounce your Jewish identity, make a profession of faith in Jesus, and be baptized. We said thank you very much, but no thank you!

The question that should be asked: How could this thinking flourish in our present-day? A saying that I read once is the most straightforward way to answer this: A sick and dead fish can flow with the current as easily with the living. The Pastor here is not the infected fish; it is the theological orientation that resulted from the infection that broke into our institutions and churches early on.

EARLY CHURCH FATHERS

As one reviews Church history, and its early fathers, one will discover doctrines, mindsets, and attitudes that were influenced by anti-Semitism. Whether we are speaking about Saint Gregory of Nyssa (335-394 A.D,) Saint Augustine (354-430 A.D.,) Saint Jerome (374-419 A.D.,) Pope Innocent III (1160/61-1216 A.D.,) and Pope Pious IV (1499-1565 C.E.)

> Pope Pious IV said, "Until today, in truth, the Jews are scandalized when they hear that God was scourged, was crucified, and that He died, holding it unworthy so much as to hear that God endured things unworthy... The Jews who deny that Messiah has come and that He is God, lies. Herod is the devil, the Jews demons; that one is King of the Jews, this one the King of demon."

Two other individuals are noteworthy, but unfortunately for the wrong reasons. One is Saint John Chrysostom (344-407 C.E.) John Chrysostom (334 A.D.-407 A.D.) was the bishop of the Church at Antioch and the greatest preacher of his day. Yet, a series of eight sermons that are well preserved spoke violently against the Jews. He said there could never be forgiveness for the Jews, that God had always hated them. He taught it was the "Christian duty" to hate the Jews. The Jews were assassins of Christ, worshipers of the devil, that their synagogue is worse than a brothel, a den of scoundrels, a temple of demons devoted to idolatrous cults."

The second individual came out of the reformation of the 1500s, Martin Luther (1483-1546.) Though he brought a needed breath of fresh air to a Church that was trapped in the Dark Ages and was concerned for the salvation of the Jewish people in his early years when they repeatedly rejected him and his message, his spirit turned to a bitter pool of anger, and resentment, and he developed a hatred for them. He began to spew this poisonous hate through sermons with zeal, drawing mental pictures with fiery words that linger in the Church and, in the minds of the Jewish people today. The following are excerpts from Martin Luther's, The Jew and Their Lies (1543.) [6]

> "What then shall we Christians do with this damned, rejected race of Jews? Since they live among us, and we know about their lying, blasphemy, and cursing, we cannot tolerate them if we do not wish to share in their lies, curses, and blasphemy. In this way, we cannot quench the inextinguishable fire of divine rage (as the prophets say) nor convert the Jews. We must prayerfully and reverentially practice a mild severity. Perhaps we may save a few from the fire and the flames. We must not seek vengeance. They are surely being punished a thousand times more than we might wish them. Let me give you my honest advice."

◆◆◆

First, their synagogues or churches should be set on fire, and whatever does not burn up should be covered or spread over with dirt so that no one may ever be able to see a cinder or stone of it. This ought to be done for the honor of God and of Christianity in order that God may see that we are Christians and that we have not wittingly tolerated or approved of such public lying, cursing, and blaspheming of His Son and His Christians.

Second, their houses should likewise be broken down and destroyed. For they perpetrate the same things there that they do in their synagogues. For this reason, they ought to be put under one roof or in a stable, like gypsies, so that they may realize that they are not masters in our land, as they boast, but miserable captives, as they complain of us incessantly before God with their bitter wailing.

Third, they should be deprived of their prayer books and Talmud's in which such idolatry, lies, cursing, and blasphemy are taught.

Fourth, their rabbis must be forbidden under threat of death to teach anymore.

Fifth, passport and traveling privileges should be forbidden to Jews, for they have no business in the rural districts since they are not nobles, nor officials, nor merchants, nor the like. Let them stay at home.

Sixth, they ought to be stopped from usury. All their cash and valuables of silver and gold ought to be taken from them and put aside for safekeeping. For this reason, as said before, everything that they possess they stole and robbed from us through their usury, for they have no other means of support. This money should be used in the case (and in no other) where a Jew has honestly become a Christian, so that he may get for the time being one or two or three hundred florins, as the person may require. This in order that he may start a business to support his poor Wife and children and the old and feeble. Such evilly acquired money is cursed, unless, with God's blessing, it is put to some useful and necessary use.

◆ ◆ ◆

The Encyclopedia Judaica comments about Luther's tract when it states, "Short of the Auschwitz oven and extermination, the whole Nazi Holocaust is pre-outlined here." 7 Is it any wonder that Hitler and Julius Streicher quoted Martin Luther as justification for their destruction of 6 million Jews?

After reading this work, our lingering focus should not be on the historical edicts, or policies that were brought about by Constantine's Christianity or the errors of such men as Martin Luther. We must instead traverse these historical mind fields and gain a greater understanding of the Jewish experience throughout Church history. I think Dr. Michael Brown sums up best the course that should be taken in; Our Hands Are Stained with Blood,

> "It is true that the Church has sinned terribly against the Jewish people, but not all the Church has sinned, wherever Jesus has been lifted up and adored, there have always been genuine lovers of Israel. There has been a bloody river of hatred that has flowed through the history of the Church. But there has also been a stream of sacrificial love. It must overflow its banks in our day. Mercy and compassion must arise for the Lord's brothers and sisters in the flesh. One could easily review the Crusades, the Spanish Inquisition, and the

Russian Pogroms. Yes, the walls of Church history are open for our inspection, but the daunting task of scaling walls of long-held misunderstanding is wonderfully accelerated". [8]

◆◆◆◆

HOW THE CROSS BECAME A SWORD

- Justin Martyr (AD 100 – AD 165) claimed that God's covenant with the Jews was no longer valid and that gentiles had replaced Jews in God's redemptive plan.

- Ignatius, the bishop of the Church in Antioch early in the second century, wrote that anyone who celebrated the Passover with the Jews, or received emblems of the Jewish feast, was a partaker with those who killed the Lord and His apostles.

- Clement of Alexandria (AD 150 – AD 215) Emphasized Greek philosophy rather than the Tanakh as the primary means God gave the gentiles to lead them to Jesus as the ultimate "Word of God."

- Tertullian (AD 160 – AD 220) was one of the most important Christian writers of the second century. His works were highly significant in developing the fundamental doctrines of the Church. In one of his writings titled Against the Jews, he blamed the entire Jewish race for the death of Jesus.

- Eusebius (AD 263 – AD 339) wrote the history of the Church for the first three centuries. He taught that the promises and blessings of the Tanakh were for the Christians and that the curses were for the Jews. He declared that the Church was the "true Israel of God" that had replaced literal Israel in God's covenants.

- John Chrysostom (AD 344 – AD 407) was the bishop of the Church at Antioch and the greatest preacher of his day. He gave a series of eight sermons in which he spoke violently against the Jews, saying there could never be forgiveness for the Jews and that God had always hated them. He taught that it was the "Christian duty" to hate the Jews. According to Chrysostom, the Jews were the assassins of Christ and worshipers of the devil.

- Jerome (AD 345 – AD 420) a great Bible scholar, his Latin translation of the Scriptures became the official Bible of the Church. Jerome claimed that the Jews were incapable of understanding the Scriptures and that they should be severely persecuted until they confessed the "true faith."

END OF CHAPTER QUESTIONS

1. The early church needed a new living organism or Christian expression apart from Judaism, Why? What was the impact on the Jewish people? What was the impact on the Church today?

2. In the eyes of many of His day, Yeshua was in fact the authentic Maschiach, and many accepted Him as the fulfillment of the Old Testament Prophets. Why then do the Jewish people reject Jesus as the Messiah? Give 6 reason that the leadership of Jesus day rejected.

3. The *Encyclopedia Judaica* comments about Luther's tract when it states, "Short of the Auschwitz oven and extermination, the whole Nazi Holocaust is pre-outlined here."[7] Is it any wonder that Hitler and Julius Streicher quoted Martin Luther as justification for their destruction of 6 million Jews? What impact does this have on Jewish ministry today? How do you think the Jewish people see the Cross in comparison to a Christian? Give six reason for each.

4. The Jewish people became viewed as the rejected people of God. A people who had lost their covenantal inheritance, and the Church viewed themselves as their replacement, the new chosen people. What forms of thinking evolved that would forever erect a wall of separation between the Jewish people and the Church?

CHAPTER EIGHT

Theological Thievery (Further Separation)

HISTORICALLY, JEWISH SENTIMENT IN THE CHRISTIAN CHURCH CAN BE PLACED IN TWO CATEGORIES: Things that separate Christians and Jews called discontinuity; and things that unite Christians and Jews, only, continuity.

When it comes to discontinuity, our attention is on a sequence of "theological pilferages." I refer to the robbing of Biblical truths and precepts, which created a historical, divide between the Jew and the Gentile. It etched its mark on the Christian Church to this day. We touch not upon such doctrines as, Salvation, Grace, Sanctification, or Eternal Life, as these doctrines are the glories of New Covenant life, of which there is no distinction between the Jew and Gentile.

The issues of discontinuity, brings us back to man's involvement in Christian history, particularly in his dealings with the Jew. Therefore, we challenge mindsets and biased decisions against Jews. Always, we are bringing to light the enemy's activity, and efforts rob from her the idea of Jewish election, as well as Jewish presence. So, let us uncover the first theft.

FIRST THEFT:
RIGHT INTERPRETIVE REASONING

In doing additional research for this chapter, I consulted Black's Law Dictionary, sixth edition, Page 1523. Unalienable is something incapable of being sold and transferred." An added meaning comes from the fundamental understanding of English Common Law, which the United States and most Commonwealth countries are heirs to, "land cannot be given away, sold, or granted to another...the land can only be inherited. A great detriment to the understanding of Scripture came about with the development of the Allegorical Interpretation of Scripture.

♦♦♦

An allegory is a work in which the characters and events represent other things and symbolically express a more in-depth, often spiritual, moral, or political meaning. Rather than interpret Scripture literally, influential individuals like Origen (185-254 AD) interpreted end-time prophecies through this allegorizing method. He obliterated the distinction between Israel and the Church, Israel and the covenant land, and the relationship between the Church and the Jewish people.

Now Origen was known as a brilliant scholar, philosopher, and one who was known to be firm in his faith and lived a genuinely humble life. But as noted earlier, his form of interpretation of symbols and spiritual meanings was overreaching. It took the reader beyond his or her literal meaning and context where no one can prove his interpretation.

With his interpretations, speculative and subjective, whose interpretation is correct? Should one rely on the most notable conference speaker at the time? Should we heed the interpretations of the most outstanding and famous author? What about the most convincing intellectual as Origen was? Perhaps it is a Eusebius type, who authored numerous volumes of work. Also, repeated throughout history by many, Origen gained influence because of his intelligence and scholarly insight. However, while those qualities are noble and essential, his ideas of biblical interpretation influenced theologians to regard the Hebrew Scriptures merely as a foreshadow of the New Testament, and Israel as a people who have lost their covenant inheritance and relationship to God.

This may be difficult to receive, but as a germ always needs a host, Institutional Christianity became the host for this form of interpretation. At the core of this was, of course, satan. Our adversary is a thief and steals what he can, which is one of his three methods of operation throughout history (John 10:10.) Often he can accomplish his plan through notable figures that can operate as angels of light, and at the same time, be used for dark purposes. Martin Luther was such an individual. We will elaborate on him further in Chapter [8].

To our topic, I have witnessed pastors on numerous times comment when discussing Biblical texts about Israel and the Jewish people and state; I know there is something unique about the Jewish people and Israel, but I do not know what it is. The awkwardness and uncertainly in one trying to understand the text plainly, particularly when it comes to Israel and the Jewish people, is often attributed to a historical root presence of allegorizing that is deeply rooted in Christian church culture. I am aware of this because I was once oriented in it.

◆ ◆ ◆

[1] Phillip Schaff: Truly, allegorizing was nothing short of a diabolical plan that intruded upon the New Covenant body, and it succeeded! Philip Schaff, the nineteenth-century church historian notes of Origen:

> "Even heathens and heretics admired or feared his brilliant talent and vast learning. His knowledge embraced all departments of the philology, philosophy, and theology of his day." 2" "Origen desires to harmonize the New Testament with the philosophy of Plato, his leaning to idealism, and His constant desire is to find a hidden mystic meaning. Though his allegorical interpretation is ingenious, it often runs away from the text and degenerates into the merest caprice." [3]

[2] Coach Bill McCarthy of the Road to Jerusalem ministry found in recent surveys that over 60% of churches in America hold to such views that allegorizing created, like replacement theology 4 (the New Testament Church is Israel, the gentile Christian is a Jew.

[3] Hal Lindsey: According to Hal Lindsey in his book, The

Road to Holocaust: "The man most responsible for changing the way the Church interpreted prophecy was Origen" A leading teacher of theology and philosophy at the influential catechetical school of Alexandria, Egypt at the beginning of the third century.

[4] A.H. Newman: Origen was the first to reduce the allegorical method of interpretation to a system... His way of Scripture interpretation was soon adopted throughout the Church and prevailed throughout the Middle Ages.

[5] Joshua Heschel (1907-1972:) Considered one of the foremost Jewish theologians of the twentieth century wrote of allegorizing: The radical use of the method of allegorizing of the Hebrew Bible, the tendency to spiritualize the meaning of its works and to minimize its plain historical sense has made many Christians incapable of understanding or having empathy for what the Holy Land means to the Jewish people and to the authors of the Hebrew Bible, or what the people of Israel means in the flesh, not just as a symbol or as a construct of theologians.

♦ ♦ ♦

ONE LAST NOTE:
ALLEGORIZING VERSUS JEWISH INTERPRETATION

Historically Jewish interpretation maintained that verse must not depart from its plain meaning. Contrary to the overreaching symbolisms and interpretations of allegorizing, Jewish understanding sees the prophetic writings and accepts them on a literal basis. Taking the reader from one reality to the next, you move amongst symbols and tangible things such as people and not abstractions as early church theology has taught.

Ironically, Judaism was not unaffected by allegorizing either. It was well known that a distinction developed between the Palestinian and Alexandrian schools of thought. Those who came from the Alexandrian schools followed the "allegorical" method of exegesis even though it was at great odds with the rulings of Jewish law.

The Talmud records in Aboth 9a, that an Alexandrian school degenerated so much from it, that the literal sense of the commandments was rejected for the symbolic. This to the extent that, circumcision, sacrifices, and holy days, were ignored, which produced a spirit of antinomianism; [] something that the body contends with today due to an unrestrained view of grace.

When I was called into full-time ministry to the Lost Sheep of Israel, it was proceeded by a His audible voice at 3:AM in the morning with a clear directive that jolted me out of my sleep. From that day forward, a series of events occurred, from leaving a lucrative career to many doors opening that confirmed our calling. But there was a period of questioning over what the Lord truly wanted me to do, especially considering my former theological orientation of replacement thinking and allegorizing. I knew that I needed a complete transformation of understanding and thought. As a result, I was led by the Lord to pray this prayer; Lord restore the eyes of my Grandfather, that is my Jewish eyes; my paternal Grandfather, who was an Orthodox Rabbi in Germany, and one that I have never had the privilege of meeting.

One morning after three months of praying fervently for this, I opened my Bible, and from my lips came, O MY God! The Lord restored the eyes of my Grandfather! I received back my Jewish eyes! Immediately, the scriptures came alive in a way that I had not experienced before, after being devoted to God's Word for years.

Instantly and miraculously, years of replacement theology and allegorizing were removed along with reformed thinking. I began to see the plan of God for Jew and Gentile, the Church, and her call to Zion in the coming days. I understood for the first time the prophetic pieces of the puzzle that I was blinded to for so long. So miraculous and complete was this understanding, I began teaching a class in a local Church that we attended, called, Israel, the Church, and the Last Days shortly after.

SECOND THEFT:
THE WIFE OF JEHOVAH

An area severely victimized by allegorizing still exists today. I refer to the identity of the Wife of Jehovah in Scripture as one example. The distinction between the "Bride of Messiah" (one comprised of both Jew and Gentile) and the "Wife of Jehovah", (consisting solely of Israel) is essential to get a full depiction of the end times regarding the relationship between Jew and the Gentile.

Traditionally, the Bride is the same as the Wife of Jehovah. But when understood this way, and Scripture is not taken literally, both the Wife and the Bride lose their distinct callings. In the New Testament, we see the distinction from Romans 11:26 "And so all Israel will be saved, as it is written: "The deliverer will come from Zion; he will turn godlessness away from Jacob." The "All Israel" is not the New Testament Gentile Church; it is the Wife of Jehovah comprised of the Jewish people as a whole, or Israel. From the Old Testament, or at times called by God, Jerusalem, as in Ezekiel 16:15-34, God speaks personally to Israel in this manner.

Though the relationship between the Jewish people and God has been tumultuous, there is a beautiful reunion that takes place as Romans indicates. Israel, the Wife of Jehovah, goes through courtship, marriage, adultery, separation, divorce, punishment, remarriage, and is finally and happily restored to a life of blessings, which Romans 11:26 promises. This is Israel's story.

Review Israel's relationship with God below. One can see the extraordinary destiny upon Israel as a nation, as the Jew begins to come into the light of God's prophetic plan.

◆ ◆ ◆

[1] The Marriage from Ezekiel 16:8: "' Later I passed by, and when I looked at you and saw that you were old enough for love, I spread the corner of my garment over you and covered your nakedness. I gave you my solemn oath and entered into a covenant with you, declares the Sovereign LORD, and you became mine."

[2] The Great Adultery from Hosea 2:2-5: "Rebuke your mother, rebuke her, for she is not my wife, and I am not her husband. Let her remove the adulterous look from her face and the unfaithfulness from between her breasts. 3 Otherwise, I will strip her naked and make her as bare as on the day she was born; I will make her like a desert, turn her into a parched land, and slay her with thirst. 4 I will not show my love to her children, because they are the children of adultery. 5 Their mother has been unfaithful and has conceived them in disgrace. Additional passages, Jeremiah 3: 1-5; 20; Ezekiel 16:15-34.)

[3] The Separation from Isaiah 50:1: "This is what the LORD says:" Where is your mother's certificate of divorce with which I sent her away? Or to which of my creditors did I sell you? Because of your sins, you were sold; because of your transgressions, your mother was sent away. "NIV

[4] The Great Divorce from Jeremiah 3: 6-10: "...During the reign of King Josiah, the LORD said to me, "Have you seen what faithless Israel has done? She has gone up on every high hill and under every spreading tree and has committed adultery there. 7 I thought that after she had done all this, she would return to me, but she did not, and her unfaithful sister Judah saw it. 8 I gave faithless Israel her certificate of divorce and sent her away because of all her adulteries. Yet I saw that her unfaithful sister Judah had no fear; she also went out and committed adultery. 9 Because Israel's immorality mattered so little to her, she defiled the land and committed adultery with stone and wood. 10 In spite of all this, her unfaithful sister Judah did not return to me with all her heart, but only in pretense," declares the LORD. NIV

[5] The Great Punishment from Ezekiel 16:35-43: "...'Therefore, you prostitute, hear the Word of the LORD! 36 This is what the Sovereign LORD says: Because you poured out your wealth and exposed your nakedness in your promiscuity with your lovers, and because of all your detestable idols, and because you gave them your children's blood, 37, therefore, I am going to gather all your lovers, with whom you found pleasure, those you loved as well as those you hated. I will gather them against you from all around and will strip you in front of them, and they will see all your nakedness. 38 I will sentence you to the punishment of women who commit adultery and who shed blood; I will bring upon you the blood vengeance of my wrath and jealous anger. 39 Then I will hand you over to your lovers, and they will tear down your mounds and destroy your lofty shrines. They will strip you of your clothes and take your fine jewelry and leave you naked and bare. 40 They will bring a mob against you, who will stone you and hack you to pieces with their swords. 41 They will burn down your houses and inflict punishment on you in the sight of many women. I will put a stop to your prostitution, and you will no longer pay your lovers. 42 Then my wrath against you will subside and my jealous anger will turn away from you; I will be calm and no longer angry. 43 '" Because you did not remember the days of your youth but enraged me with all these things, I will surely bring down on your head what you have done, declares the Sovereign LORD. Did you not add lewdness to all your other detestable practices? (See Hosea 2:6-13.)

[6] The Great Remarriage and Restored Blessings from Ezekiel 16: 60-63: "Yet I will remember the covenant I made with you in the days of your youth, and I will establish an everlasting covenant with you. 61 Then you will remember your ways and be ashamed when you receive your sisters, both those who are older than you and those who are younger. I will give them to you as daughters, but not on the basis of my covenant with you. 62 So I will establish my covenant with you, and you will know that I am the LORD. 63 Then, when I make atonement for you for all you have done, you will remember and be ashamed and never again open your mouth because of your humiliation, declares the Sovereign LORD.'" (See Isaiah 54:1-8; 62:4-5; Hosea 2:14-23.)

THIRD THEFT:
OUR DISTINCTION

Throughout the Biblical period, the term nation (a Hebrew idiom) commonly refers to Jews, not gentiles. It is true that every people group and nation comprise the ethnos, the Greek term for nations in our modern thought. But the Bible states something different about the Jew.

The Word gentile is continually derived from goy or goyim is its plural...and almost always, it refers to a non-Israelite, a foreign non-Jew, the heathen or nations. In the book of Leviticus 20:26, it states, "You are to be holy to me because I, the LORD, am holy, and I have set you apart from the nations to be my own."

Deuteronomy 4:19-20 warns Israel not to worship the things He has given the nations, but he states, "But as for you", the Lord brought you out of Egypt to be a people of His inheritance." Luke 21:10-11 states, "Nation [ethnos] will rise against nation [ethnos] and kingdom against kingdom." It refers to the nation against nation, kingdom against kingdom, and is a Hebrew idiom for World Wars—not small regional border disputes or skirmishes.

The Luke passage reinforces Jewish writings about the end times. In the Bereshit Rabbah, it states, "If you see kingdom (nation) rise against one another, then give heed to the footsteps of Messiah." In James 1:1, "To the twelve tribes scattered among the nations..." Here, the term "nations" is speaking about the Jewish Diaspora at the time (Israelite residents in gentile countries.)

Finally, in Galatians 3:8, the word "heathen" brings us back to the Word ethnos, which indicates foreigners or non-Jews; "And the Scripture, foreseeing that God would justify the heathen through faith, preached before the gospel unto Abraham, saying, in thee shall all nations be blessed.

FOURTH THEFT:
TO THE JEW FIRST

The words of Isaiah point to John the Baptist's work of course as a spiritual one, "every mountain and hill shall be made low: and the crooked shall be made straight and the rough places plain" (Isaiah 40:3-4.) Of course, once the spiritual highway was built, it would lead to every corner of the earth from Jerusalem out. Messiah came for the redemption of Israel for sure, but also for the salvation of the nations. Still, salvation was always to go to the Jew first.

In Matthew 10:5-6, Yeshua lays down this evangelistic model; "Do not go among the Gentiles or enter any town of the Samaritans. Go to the "lost sheep of Israel." It is repeated in Romans 1:16, "I am not ashamed of the gospel, because it is the power of God for the salvation of everyone who believes: first for the Jew, then for the Gentile."

This offering of the kingdom to Israel is their right to choose or their right of first refusal. Israel's right to receive the offering of the kingdom first is because Israel was God's firstborn son, according to Exodus 4:22, which is a distinction not made to any other for one. Second, it was God's design to go to the Jew first.

Third, the Jew must, in the future, choose their Messiah for the Messianic Kingdom to begin.

♦ ♦ ♦

In other words, the prerequisite of the second coming rests upon the shoulders of the Jewish people. Yeshua establishes this truth in several places.

One place is in Matthew "For I tell you, you will not see me again until you say, "Blessed is he who comes in the name of the Lord" (Matthew 23:39.) Then Luke, "Look, your house is left to you desolate. I tell you; you will not see me again until you say," Blessed is he who comes in the name of the Lord" (Luke 13:35.) Finally, in Hosea 5:15, "Then I will go back to my place until they admit their guilt. And they will seek my face; in their misery, they will earnestly seek me."

When we discuss the principle of "First," the gentile Church has traditionally seen it as a past pattern, or a historic startup model that was used only to begin the Church. The practical function of this fostered the idea that the Jews were first then, but due to their rejection of their Messiah two thousand years ago, the gentiles are now first. Later at the close of the age, God will again turn His attention to the Jew. Hence, the Jew is no longer first, but last!

MORE ON "FIRST"

When exploring this principle of "first" further, we find that it was always dynamic and forward speaking, and never was it static. "First" comes from the Greek Word proton (pro'-ton,) meaning first in time, place, and order of importance.

Scientifically, a proton carries an inherent positive electric charge. Without it, an atom cannot form. For this reason, the Greeks saw it as "the" fundamental component of the universe. Spiritually and prophetically, this speaks powerfully to the Jew and the gentile body even today. The Jew was chosen first in time and place. In the building of the New Covenant body they are God's firstborn and the elder brother. In the age to come, right relationships will finally be restored, including, the relationship between Isaac and Ishmael, Jew, and Arab. Also, the relationship between the Jew and Gentile (first and second born.

Hence, as the Jew was the fundamental building component of the body, something else comes into view from Romans 11:15; "If their rejection [speaking of the Jews] is the reconciliation of the world, what will their acceptance be but life from the dead?" From this passage, the body is depicted as deprived of life and needs to be revived.

How will this revival come?

It will come by way of the Jew! It portrays the return of the Jew as a spiritual defibrillator. A defibrillator sends an electric charge across the surface of a heart that has stopped. For sure, the Gentile Church has lived with the glories of New Covenant life and the Spirit for 2000 years. She has received glorious visitations and revivals while proclaiming the gospel to the four corners of the world. But the return of the Jewish people will usher in a quality of life that will dwarf all past glories.

Again, here is the passage from Romans 11:15, "For if their rejection is the reconciliation of the world, what will their acceptance be but life from the dead?" Yes, Yeshua had to come to His own for His own to turn Him away (John 1:11; Isaiah 53.) He had to suffer for righteousness sake, and that all generations; Jew and Gentile could be saved (John 1:12.)

Still, the model of first-things-first-evangelism is set: "Do not go among the Gentiles or enter any town of the Samaritans. Go to the lost sheep of Israel" (Matthew 10:5-6.) "...I am not ashamed of the gospel, because it is the power of God for the salvation of everyone who believes: first for the Jew, then for the Gentile" (Romans 1:16.

END OF CHAPTER QUESTIONS

1. Describe the Wife of Jehovah relationship with God? Give Scriptural references of the stages of the Jewish people's relationship with God?

2. How was the distinction stolen from the Jewish people?

3. What role did the church have in displacing the identity of the Jew and Israel?

4. Explain, to the "Jew First"?

5. What is Allegorical Interpretation, and who was its founder?

CHAPTER NINE

Sabbath and Torah
"Coming to A Common Understanding"

MANY ARE COMING TO THE LIGHT OF SATURDAY-SABBATH TODAY, the 4th commandment to rest on the seventh-day and honor the Lord.

At the end of any dialogue and debate on this hot topic, the believer must choose freely by God's grace and liberty what direction they should take. Praise God that our salvation and the means to righteousness are no longer determined by it. There is only one way to attain righteousness, and that is through the sacrificial work of our Messiah alone.

With Hebraic streams flowing today, many are in the process of navigating this issue of Saturday Sabbath. So, we will touch on some of the major quakes that shook the Jewish and Christian world, particularly with its influence on Sabbath. Also, we will surface the age-old debate between Sunday Sabbath and Saturday.

ROMAN CHRISTIANITY, JEWS, And SABBATH

The architect of Roman Christianity, or the beginning of the Catholic Church, was Emperor Constantine, which we continually return in our journey. Considered the first Pope of the new Catholic Church following his conversion to Christianity, he instituted Sunday as the official day of rest. This conversion was also beneficial to him because he was able to retain pagan practices for years, which included the worship of the Roman sun god Mithra; Sunday was the Roman day of worship of this god and came from the Latin dies Solis, or sun's day.

Constantine's edicts and legislations on Sunday as the new Sabbath in his Edict of Tolerance were devastating on the Torah, and then, of course, the Jews. With the Greek's interpretation of the word Torah, one could say that the Greeks built the coffin, and Constantine nailed it shut. Soon the early church fathers began to see themselves as purging Sabbath from Jewish falsehood while having the chance to infuse it with a new faith and freedom.

When it comes to Christian teaching, traditionally speaking, it became based upon the pattern of the early Jewish believers gathering on Sunday mornings as already cited. Most agree that following our Lord's ascension, the early believers began gathering on Sunday the first day of the week, which became known as the "Lords Day" (Revelation chapter 1.)

This issue, however, is still debated and remains the

historical rub. Was Sunday an added day called The Lord's Day, or was it a substitute for Saturday Shabbat, which originated from the fourth commandment? "For in six days the Lord made heaven and earth, the sea, and all that is in them, and rested on the seventh day; wherefore the Lord blessed the Sabbath day and hallowed it" (Exodus 20:11.)

We can only say that historically speaking, the church's need for another official Sabbath was essential to craft a model absent of Jews and Judaism. The fact that the Jew and Judaism were seen as a rejected people and religion, particularly following the destruction of the temple in 70 AD by the Roman armies, is no small influence.

◆ ◆ ◆

Following these events, the Jew's entire ecclesiastical system became invalidated in the minds of early Church fathers. They interpreted it as God's judgment on the Jews and Judaism. But this was not the case, praise God!

Given this historical and ecclesiastical error, Saturday observance would have legitimized the Jewish Sabbath of this so-called rejected religion. And if the Jew observed Sunday Sabbath, it would have legitimized Christianity as a replacement of Judaism. And compounding this, Sunday observance on the part of the early Jewish believers would have abolished the very Torah. Clearly, once the Jewish root was severed, an abyss was cut between Judaism and Christianity that became irreconcilable.

PAUL and SABBATH

When discussing Saturday Sabbath in light of a deeply rooted Orthodox Jew as the Apostle Paul, abandoning the 7th day Sabbath would have violated the Torah, let alone deny one's very identity as a Jew. Josephus, the Jewish historian, writes, "violating the Sabbath" was one of the greatest hallmarks of covenant disloyalty" (Jewish Antiquities 11.346.) [1]

To understand Paul's words on Sabbath, holy days, and law, one must first discover him in the book of Acts. It is one of the best places to meet Paul, the Jew, and understand the context of all future remarks. Too often, we draw our conclusions solely from the context of a specific book and lose the individual. Paul in Acts 24:14, is addressing certain rumors of him breaking the Jewish laws. Paul states, "They cannot prove to you the charges they are making against me." He further says, "I believe everything that agrees with the Law."

Then in chapter 25, verses 8, Paul states, "I have done nothing wrong against the law of the Jews or against the temple or Caesar." Finally, in a climactic conversation that takes place between Paul and the brothers who were fellow Jews, he states, "from morning till evening he explained and declared to them the kingdom of God, and tried to convince them about Jesus from the Law of Moses and the Prophets."

It would not be possible for Paul to make such arguments as the ones shown if he was violating the most fundamental principles of the Torah, notably if he had replaced Saturday with Sunday. A contemporary of Paul, Philo, writes these words on Sabbath, "The sacred seventh day, exceeding sanctity and purity, a time to regulate one's conduct towards God by the rules and piety and holiness, and one's conduct towards men by the rules of humanity and justice." 2

Then we have the use of Sabbath in the New Testament. "The Sabbath" refers to "The" Sabbath day, not numerous sabbaths and holy days as is spoken of over forty times in the New International Version. Paul often speaks of "The Sabbath" in the context of the pervasive legalism that existed. Some thirty-nine different kinds of work were forbidden on Sabbath. One can only imagine what Paul was facing when he spoke of it, and being surrounded by rabbis who were ingenious legalists,

> No...Grinding, sifting, dyeing, beating, making two cords, weaving two threads, separating two strands, making a knot of two strands, beating smooth with a hammer. And these have further restrictions on their range and meaning. [3]

In the following, Paul is again speaking of Sabbaths, festivals, meats, drinks, and New Moons. Our focus is upon the Sabbath in light of this most familiar passage, "Therefore, do not let anyone judge you by what you eat or drink, or concerning a religious festival, a New Moon celebration or a Sabbath day. These are a shadow of the things that were to come; the reality, however, is found in Christ" (Galatians 2:19 NIV.) From this passage, many say that man is no longer under the law of the commandments, and since we are now in the age of Grace, the Sabbath is no longer required.

Paul is not referring to "The Sabbath" for reasons that we have already stated. Paul does state that he died to the law in Romans 7:4 so that he may live for God and be joined to the Messiah. The laws that Paul died to pertains to animal sacrifices for sure, the mediation of a high priest, the yoke that strangled the people with all the legal disciplines that were supposed to lead the Jewish people to the "Living Torah."

♦♦♦

Romans chapter 14:5 & 6, which some cite as an argument against the Saturday Sabbath-keeping states, "One man considers one day more sacred than another; another man considers every day alike. Each one should be fully convinced in his own mind. He who regards one day as special does so to the Lord. He who eats meat, eats to the Lord, for he gives thanks to God; and he who abstains, does so to the Lord and gives thanks to God.

These special days that are spoken are specific "fast' days that were instituted by the prophets. Paul seeks to establish crucial instructions as a result of their immaturity, divisions, and judgments regarding these man-made days. He wants to lay down necessary guidelines for them. But the entire context of chapter 14 is clearly dealing with meats, specific foods, and fasts.

To the Greeks and Romans, culturally speaking, Sabbath was viewed with disdain. Sabbath was, in fact, a target of ridicule and humor as roman satirists made Sabbath a theme of one-line jokes. The famous Stoic philosopher and moralist

Seneca wrote about Sabbath,

> "Jewish superstition, especially the Sabbath, is reprehensible, for by refusing to work every seventh day, they [the Jews] lose the seventh part of their life in idleness, and important matters are neglected." [4]

One cannot avoid the topic of the Septuagint when discussing "The" Sabbath. The Greek translation of the Hebrew Bible was produced in 250 BCE. But when the Greeks undertook this assignment, it is well documented that there was no equivalent word in the Greek language for the Hebrew word for Torah, (yarah). In the Hebrew, yarah, means instruction, to hit the mark, or to point out.

When they opted for the closest Greek word nomos, it took on a robust legalistic sense that equated to law. This word nomos is used 190 times in the New Testament. It refers to the law of God; the law of the Spirit of life in Yeshua; the law of sin and death; the law of righteousness, works of the law; end of the law;, book of the law; and the curse of the law.[5]

With our western concept, nomos, came to imply a burdensome and legalistic set of rules and regulations. This gives the notion that one is no longer obligated to even obey the Ten Commandments...the fourth commandment to honor the 7th day Sabbath for example. In some circles today, the fourth commandment of the Ten Commandments is viewed as returning to the law.

Yet, the New Testament states that the law is "Good." That is, not as legalistic yoke or a means to righteousness. (I Timothy

1:8.) Again, the law is "Holy" and "Spiritual" (Romans 7:12.) Though our salvation is no longer dependent upon any observance of the law (I am speaking of the Ten Commandments,) the redemptive life with its accompanying grace and freedom compels us to obey these commandments that Moshe (Moses) received on Sinai.

For instance, it remains the Father's will for us to honor our father and mother, to not covet our neighbor's wife, or take the Lord's name in vain. We, in like manner, honor the Sabbath and rest on the Seventh-day to praise the Lord. These are universal principles that are found in God's moral code for man in his journey through life. In these, Torah life remains relevant for man today.

MORE from PAUL on SABBATH

Paul's concern is always freedom, especially following the sacrificial work of Yeshua and the outpouring of the Spirit on Pentecost (Shavuot.) I believe Paul lived each day seeking to imbue old Jewish life with the Spirit, which included the fourth commandment. He recognized the chance to move the Torah into the realm of the heart, and not cancel it.

This heart issue is something that that Messiah continually taught about, "if one lusts in his heart for another woman, he has committed adultery (Matthew 5:28.) Doesn't this touch upon the core of any observance? If the law, speaking of the commandment of Sabbath observance, becomes a means to righteousness, and becomes more important than the liberty of the spirit, grace is diminished, and a return to righteousness through the law creeps in. Yet, Paul maintains that the law is good (1Timothy 1:8.)

To conclude, God did not nail the Sabbath observance to the cross. He nailed the legal requirement of Sabbath rite to the cross. We observe Sabbath out of our obedience to God's word, not as a means to righteousness—Our justification comes only through the blood of our Messiah and God's grace alone. On a historical note, Edward Sinan writes of the Torah in The Popes and the Jews:

> "There is no moment…when Christian legislation on the Jews is silent on the providential role, especially as guardians of Scripture. Pope Innocent III (1198-1216) exemplifies this spiritual dependence of Christianity on the Jews in an address to the count of Nevers, where he argues that the Jews ought not to be slain lest the Christian people forget divine law.'…The notion of Jews functioning to remind Christians of the Law presumes their existence, not as potential converts, but precisely as Jew." [6]

Lastly, consider Isaiah's words, which are apt reminders of God's long-held intention for the Jew, with a beautiful invitation to the gentile with regards to Sabbath-keeping as well, "

> Blessed is the man who does this, the man who holds it fast, who keeps the Sabbath without desecrating it, and keeps his hand from doing any evil"

(Isaiah 56:2.)

"If you keep your feet from breaking the Sabbath and from doing as you please on my holy day if you call the Sabbath a delight and the Lord's holy day honorable, and if you honor it by not going your own way and not doing as you please or speaking idle words, then you will find your joy in the Lord, and I will cause you to ride on the heights of the land and to feast on the inheritance of your father, Jacob. The mouth of the Lord has spoken."

(Isaiah 58:13.)

"And foreigners who bind themselves to the LORD to serve him, to love the name of the LORD, and to worship him, all who keep the Sabbath without desecrating it and who hold fast to my covenant — these I will bring to my holy mountain and give them joy in my house of prayer."

(Isaiah 56:6.)

TORAH FOR TODAY

When it comes to Torah, and the Jew, their thought life and principles for living were shaped by it. From the Mishnah, Avoth (Chapters of the Fathers,) it states that when Moses received the Law from Sinai and handed it down to Joshua, then to the elders, from the elders to the prophets and the prophets to the assembly of men; it established three things:

1. Be deliberate in judgments.
2. Raise many disciples.
3. Make a fence around the Law.

In sum, Guard the Torah because it is the vital connection between God and the Jewish people. Thus, the Torah always preserved the way for generations. And today, the absolute need for God's Word in the believer's life is essential as never before; this, of course, speaks of the written Torah, and most importantly, the "Living Torah," Yeshua.

As the world sits in the crossroads of social, economic, and political reform, or revolutions, federal and global formulas are seeding the earth for a new global, economic, and societal future. More importantly, it is seeding the world for anti-messiah's government. Even as I write this book, America has faltered for the first time in her international credit rating due to her financial folly. With more financial convulsions to come, the people of God will need strategic initiatives from the throne room of Heaven. Our young must deal with this new world, and we must get it right to help them navigate the dangers ahead.

♦ ♦ ♦

In today's times, the body of believers could use ancient principles like these to recall how we are to love and revere God as this is our call—a calling that is as pervasive as the command to obey Him: "Hear, O Israel! The LORD is our God; the LORD is one! You shall love the LORD your God with all your heart, with all your soul, and with all your might. These words, which I am commanding you today, shall be on your heart" (Deuteronomy 6:4-6 NIV.)

The same passage in verses 7-9 teaches, "we must diligently teach our children to love God and to know His ways, to help mold our children's thoughts and actions through the teaching His Word, both when arising and going to bed, when walking on the street, or when going about our affairs."

END OF CHAPTER QUESTIONS

1. Who was the architect of Roman Christianity that became the basis for Institutional Christianity?

2. Explain Institutional Christianity, and provide 6 characteristics?

3. Providing Acts 24:14, 25:14 as a reference, how does it prove that Paul did not stop honoring the Saturday Sabbath?

4. What was the general view of the Roman world in Paul's day of the Sabbath? Explain Philo's remarks?

5. Explain the meaning of Torah?

CHAPTER TEN

Misconceptions and Restorations (John the Baptist and Elijah)

WE WILL TAKE JOHN OUT OF THE ROMAN CITADEL AND TRANDITIOHNAL CHRISTIAN view, where we meet a devout Jewish man who understood the hour that was dawning upon the nation of Israel, the hour of Judaism's fulfillment!

For more than 35 years of knowing my Messiah, Bible College, and hearing the Word preached by numerous teachers, seldom is John given the center of attention. Perhaps it is due to the more considerable attention of his cousin Yeshua. Most likely, it is from the systematic sanitizing of Jewish-ness from the New Testament. Greek Hellenistic thinking has long obscured John the Baptist (Yochanan,) particularly his relationship to Elijah, and his essential role in Yeshua's first phase of ministry.

When John began his public ministry nearly immediately, the multitudes were drawn to him. So great was his popularity that Josephus the Jewish historian records that Herod feared killing John due to his fear of the public. When Herod ordered John to be beheaded, the masses saw the destruction of Herod's army as a judgment from God for doing so. Still, no other Bible character gained so much attention in such a limited period than John. He came forth into public life to witness great multitudes from every quarter of the region, including Yeshua himself;

> "People went out to him from Jerusalem and all Judea and the whole territory of the Jordan. Confessing their sins, they were baptized by him in the Jordan River. Then Jesus came from Galilee to the Jordan to be baptized by John. But John tried to deter him, saying, "I need to be baptized by you, and do you come to me?"
>
> (Matthew 3:5-6, 13-14.)

HIS BIRTH and COMING

Scripture reveals that John the Baptist came forth from the desert and the wilderness. He grew strong in the spirit until he began his public ministry to Israel (Luke1.) His father Zechariah was from the line of Abia or Abijah a priestly line (1 Chronicles 24:10,) and his mother Elizabeth, was one of the daughters of Aaron (Luke 1:5.) Luke reveals that John's father was filled with the Holy Spirit when he prophesied of their long-awaited Messiah and about his son John (1:67-59.)

John was a devout and zealous Jew, perhaps a former member of the Essenes. He would be considered a strange and unusual fellow today as he was then; "he wore clothing made of camel's hair and a leather belt around his waist, and he ate locusts and wild honey" (Mark 1:6.)

However, prophets can be somewhat different from others. They are less inhibited and concerned with what others think.

They can call out the sins of the people when the average person would be fearful and hesitant. It makes them reliable partners with God.

VIEWING JOHN CORRECTLY

To see John in the context of our study, we must consider him in the context of Jewish history that was coming to its climactic point. Rav Shaul states, "But when the time had fully come to God sent his Son, born of a woman, born under the laws, to redeem those under the law, that we might receive the full rights of sons" (Galatians 4:4-5.) John's ministry was brief. It virtually ended upon the baptism of Yeshua. John himself acknowledged, "He must increase, but I must decrease" (John 3:30 KJV.)

Still, John springs onto the scene of biblical history as a relatively unknown. Only that a whirlwind of prophetic events had begun, the long-anticipated kingdom of heaven was breaking forth onto the earth. His public life began at the end of a period that had experienced four centuries of prophetic stillness; Malachi is the last. Historians call this period the 400 years of silence.

When John emerged at the end of this Old Covenant period, just when the New Covenant period was about to begin, it was of great consequence as Israel had slipped into a state of hopelessness. Malachi states that they had turned away from God," You have said harsh things against me, declares the Lord" (Malachi 3:13.)

But notably, the Israelites had endured much at this point. When Pompey conquered Jerusalem in 63 BCE and established Roman rule, he brought high taxes and rampant idolatry. Alexander the Great ruled prior from 356-323 BCE, and though he lived a short life, Geek culture was born, giving rise to an international language, Greek. Through it, the Gospel would advance to the nations.

When the Roman Empire rose to power, an expansive road network was established that would make it possible for the systematic spread of the Gospel. Although the 400 years between Malachi and John were considered silent, they were laying the foundation for the kingdom to come.

As Greek culture permeated society, and Rome's power and culture permeated the day, Israel was longing for a King David or a Joshua type deliverer. We see this in John 6: 14-1 when Yeshua performs a miracle that caused the people to recognize him as the Prophet that was to come into the world. Jesus knowing their thoughts immediately, and it was not God's plan for him to be king; Yeshua quickly withdrew from the people.

Reclaiming John's Jewish identity and his calling, one must first be aware of how his ministry later became severely limited due to Christian misconceptions. The basis for this lies in the belief that he came to start Christianity, and baptize Gentiles into Christianity. Upon the least challenged is the notion that he came to start the New Testament Church. Yet, John comes upon the scene, not as the innovator of baptism, or the herald of Christianity, and indeed, he was not Catholic!

John was with the Lord in glory long before the Church began.

Second, the model of the Church today, or Institutional Christianity, was never a Jewish concept. So, let us start with what John is most famous for, Baptism.

BAPTISM: MIKVAH

A common misconception comes from the notion that baptism through immersion was a Christian innovation. But baptism was a Jewish practice called mikvah (Hebrew for baptism.) Scholars are uncertain where John was influenced in its administration. Still, some believe that John may have been a member of the Essenes, a sect in the Qumran community that pulled back from society to study the Torah and await the coming of the Messiah.

In the Essene community, immersion took place daily. These were "mikvah practitioners" called tovelei shaharit or "dawn bathers." Still, other Jewish groups also observed immersion to ensure their readiness for the coming of the Messiah. Even in our modern-day, the mikvah is observed in the Jewish faith for anyone undergoing ritual bath, women following menstruation and childbirth, men seeking to achieve ritual purity, or gentiles converting to Judaism.

The point is. Baptism through immersion was a common practice, and John, therefore, is never questioned about the practice. There was one issue over baptism, but it was over whose name people were being baptized in. Paul's writings to the Corinthians addresses this: "Were you baptized into the name of Paul? I am thankful that I did not baptize any of you except Crispus and Gaius, so no one can say that you were baptized into my name. Yes, I also baptized the household of Stephanas; beyond that, I do not remember if I baptized anyone else.(1 Corinthians 1:13–16.)

JOHN'S PURPOSE in COMING

Another misunderstanding was over his purpose in coming itself. Here we must stress John's national focus on Israel, which is equivalent to the emphasis of Messiah's earliest work. John states," The reason I came baptizing with water was that he might be revealed to Israel" (John 1:31.) This can be illustrated in the account of a Greek woman who came to Yeshua for healing for her daughter. Her daughter had a demon, and the mother knew that Yeshua was the only one who could genuinely help her daughter.

In the following passage, Matthew 15:23-24, the gentiles are referred to like dogs, and the children refer to the nation of Israel and the Jews,

> "But He did not answer her a word. And His disciples came and implored Him, saying, "Send her away because she keeps shouting [a]at us." But He answered and said, "I was sent only to the lost sheep of the house of Israel."

Then from the following,

> "First let the children eat all they want," he told her, "for it is not right to take" the children's bread

and toss it to their dogs." Yes, Lord," she said; even the dogs under the table eat the children's crumbs."

(Mark 7:27-28.)

Throughout John's preaching, the subject of his focus was the coming of the Messiah, and the kingdom coming to earth. The Talmud speaks of Malachi 3, and unknowingly describes John the Baptist with high accuracy, but they see another figure in it; "Who will come to usher in the Messianic Age and he will not abrogate justly established laws, but only those arbitrary and lawless decisions" (Tractate Eduyyoth 9b.) 2.

The prophecies of ancient times, particularly the words of Isaiah are also important: "A voice of one calling: "In the desert prepare the way for the LORD; make straight in the wilderness a highway for our God. (Isaiah 40:3-5.)

Also, the words of the prophet Malachi: "See, I will send my messenger, who will prepare the way before me" (Malachi 3:1.) We notice throughout that John came to build a spiritual highway, first for the nation of Israel. John did not come to prepare for a new religion or establish denominations.

John is a forerunner, a preparer for the Greater One, had the job of getting the nation of Israel ready for Yeshua 's first focus. Yeshua begins His work with Israel by trying to relax the priesthood, revealing new spiritual garments in exchange for the old garments of the law, and for them to recognize their Messiah. These spiritual newborn garments were to bring a new life of spiritual freedom, which Israel would need to carry forth

God's Word to the nations, and points to their prophetic destiny. The prophet Malachi points to this:

> "For he will be like a refiner's fire or a launderer's soap. He will sit as a refiner and purifier of silver; he will purify the Levites and refine them like gold and silver."
>
> (Malachi 3:2-3.)

Continually, John and Yeshua are trying to get Israel to cross over into the New Covenant period. It is New Covenant Judaism, as Dr. Daniel Juster calls it, a new sect of Judaism seeking to demonstrate that Yeshua was indeed the Jewish Messiah—this speaks implicitly to the value and purpose of John's coming.

JOHN AND THE KINGDOM

To cast more light on John, is to understand the kingdom, and how John understood it. The kingdom to John was not something one receives at the end of man's natural days in heaven. The kingdom to the Jew was a geopolitical entity, a government that would be led by the Messiah, and would restore national Israel.

Kingdom in Hebrew means dominion, empire, or realm. The phrase "the kingdom of heaven is near," in Matthew 3:1-2, is seen by many as a dispensational term that refers to Messiah's kingdom on earth. Others see the kingdom of heaven as a reference to heaven itself. It is the kingdom of heaven as the spiritual rule of God in the hearts of individuals whose lives are changed by the sacrificial work of the Messiah. This view makes the kingdom of heaven synonymous with the kingdom of God, a topic we have already discussed.

Dispensationalists teach that the kingdom was postponed for two millennia until God's work is complete amongst the gentiles. Still, there is the kingdom of heaven as the divine government to come on earth. To the Jew, this is the moment that had dawned upon Israel. Praise God this moment will begin again in the future, but only after the New Covenant body has returned to co-reign with Messiah to rule over cities of nations [3] in the Messianic Kingdom (See the chapter on Unlocking Israel's Election. In the Gospels, both the "kingdom of heaven" and the "kingdom of God," is referred to several times.

In the Sermon on the Mount, Yeshua teaches that those who follow the Beatitudes will gain the kingdom of God in inheriting the earth. Then in Matthew 19, the Lord compares eternal life and salvation with entering the kingdom of God, when it is upon the earth: "And he opened his mouth, and taught them, saying, Blessed are the poor in spirit: for theirs is the kingdom of heaven" (Matthew 5:2-3.)

Still, questions abound regarding John's life, especially his association with Elijah: Was John Elijah? Did John fulfill the ministry of Elijah? What common elements did John share with Elijah? We will focus on this in Part II.

PART II

Was John Elijah? Many wondered if John came to fulfill the ministry of the prophet Elijah, this is an area of confusion and debate today. In some ways, John did, but in other ways, he did not.

First, there is the erroneous belief that God no longer has a plan for Israel, and John fulfilled Malachi's prediction, thus making Elijah's ministry no-longer necessary. But this converts Elijah's ministry into an exclusively gentile Christian mission and expunges the national Jewish-Israel focus. In other words, upon Israel's non-acceptance of Messiah, God canceled His first offering to Israel. Anti-Jewish thinking abounds here that interrupts the true meaning again. Here is the prophecy of Malachi,

> "See, I will send you the prophet Elijah before that great and dreadful day of the LORD comes. He will turn the hearts of the fathers to their children, and the hearts of the children to their fathers; or else I will come and strike the land with a curse."
>
> (Malachi 4:5-6.)

Malachi provides a beautiful picture of a future restoration, where the hearts of the children will be reconnected to their Biblical forefathers, Abraham, Isaac, and Jacob. Many interpret "great and dreadful day" to be the Great Tribulation or Jacob's Trouble, and that this prophetic restoration takes place sometime before this period of great trial to come upon the earth; I happen to agree personally and theologically. Many also teach that God is going to bring about a significant restoration between natural fathers and their children. Scriptures, however, cannot support this view. Scripture teaches the opposite, and this is clear from the passages from Matthew 10:35,

> "For I have come to turn "a man against his father, a daughter against her mother, a daughter-in-law against her mother-in-law—a man's enemies will be the members of his household." Anyone who loves his father or mother more than me is not worthy of me; anyone who loves his son or daughter more than me is not worthy of me, and anyone who does not take his cross and follow me is not worthy of me." "I tell you, on that night two people will be in one bed; one will be taken and the other left. Two women will be grinding grain together; one will be taken and the other left."
>
> (Luke 17:33-35.)

Many see the words of Malachi in the context of this Hebraic restoration, whereby millions of God's children are supernaturally reintroduced to the "heart" and "substance" of the true Biblical forefathers; Abraham, Isaac, and Jacob. But wherever one stands in this restorative stream or this incredible passage, one fact remains. A movement that fans a real affection for Israel and the Jewish people, and continually provokes the gentiles back to the Jewish root, is one that originates from the heavenly realms, and certainly not from our adversary—Why would satan be divided against himself?

FOR SOME JOHN WAS ELIJAH

Continually, the people were asking John, who are you? Are you Elijah?" He rightfully responded, "I am not." "Are you the Prophet?" He answered, "No." Finally, they asked him again, "Who are you? Give us an answer to take back to those who sent us. What do you say about yourself?" John rightfully replied in the words of Isaiah the prophet, "I am the voice of one calling in the desert, 'Make straight the way for the Lord'" (John 1:21-23.)

When placing the above passage in the context of the previous verse (v. 20,), it becomes clear that they were wondering if he was the Christ. John answered three questions correctly and unmistakably draws their attention to the prophet Isaiah in chapter 40:3 to confirm the prophecy in Malachi 3; "I am a voice of one calling in the desert, 'Prepare the way of the Lord." In another place, we see the same emphasis, but something else is added,

> "I tell you the truth: Among those born of women, there has not risen anyone greater than John the Baptist. Yet, he who is least in the kingdom of heaven is greater than he is. From the days of John, the Baptist until now, the kingdom of heaven has been forcefully advancing, and forceful men lay hold of it. For all the Prophets and the Law prophesied until John. And if

you are willing to accept it, he is the Elijah who was to come. He, who has ears, let him hear."

(Matthew 11:11-5.)

Let me repeat verse fourteen. "If you are willing to accept it, he is the Elijah." Did they accept it? No. Therefore, to national Israel, John did not become their Elijah. However, to every Jew that believed John, they would have automatically accepted Yeshua, and in turn, receive the restorative work of Elijah. In this, John and Elijah share these common restorative elements. We see this in Mark 9:11-13. Messiah is speaking to His talmidim (disciples) after they had asked Him about this relationship,

> "Why do the teachers of the law say that Elijah must come first?" Jesus replied, "To be sure, Elijah does come first, and restores all things. Why then is it written that the Son of Man must suffer much and be rejected? But I tell you, Elijah has come, and they have done to him everything they wished, just as it is written about him."

From the above words, John fulfills the work of Elijah for those who were always willing to accept him. This again based on Matthew's words in 11:11-15: "...And if you are willing to accept it, he is the Elijah, who was to come. He, who has ears, let him hear."

To conclude, John came to prepare the way for the Messiah's first agenda of His ministry; go to the nation of

Israel that the righteousness of God's Word would be fulfilled. John came not to plant the early church to establish Christianity, or look for gentiles to baptize into Christianity. Yet in the process of his ministry, many gentiles came and were immersed in the kingdom.

WHAT IF?

Have you ever considered the what would have happened if Israel had accepted Yeshua two thousand years ago? Indeed, Rome would have prohibited any form of national redemption of Israel if it required allegiance to a competing King. In the word of Nathaniel, who declared in John 1:49 about Yeshua, "you are the King of Israel."

Imagine the Roman authorities listening to those words at the time. Still, let us recline as we do on Passover night and ponder the possibilities. We suddenly discover those things were lost at Messiah's first advent and those that will be restored upon His second return. So again, what if Israel had accepted the Messiah?

- The kingdom would have had its national beginning with Israel. Instead, it began in the hearts of the nations and had an "international" start.
- National Israel would have been redeemed, and all Israel would have received their Messiah. Instead, individual Jews have been coming to faith ever since, while Israel is awaiting its national restoration and glory.
- The priesthood would have been refined, and the kingdom

on earth established. Further, the hearts of the Jewish people would have been restored to their forefathers, and Elijah's work fulfilled. Elijah's work will fully occur in the future when all Israel is saved.

- Finally, the Jewish root would have stayed connected to New Covenant faith, something that will be restored in the kingdom to come.

In the future, Institutional Christianity will be eradicated upon Messiah's coming, and God's people will enter into the context of a Hebraic foundation that returns to the Biblical holy days. As we ponder such things as the prophets did at the River Chebar in Babylon, let's pray and groan for this order to be established upon this earth. These words, "We know that the whole creation has been groaning as in the pains of childbirth right up to the present time (Romans 8:22 NIV.)

END OF CHAPTER QUESTIONS

1. What was John the Baptists primary mission? Why was he called a forerunner (Matt 3:3; Malachi 3:1; Isaiah 40:3.)

2. What sect of Judaism is John believed to come from, and what does this say about the character of his Jewish identity?

3. What was the length of John actual ministry and explain some reasons for its short duration?

4. What is the relationship of John's ministry to the prophet Elijah? In what ways does John fulfill them and in what does it not.

5. Provide six examples of what would have happened if Israel had recognized Jesus as their long-awaited Messiah?

CHAPTER ELEVEN

The Gentiles Find Their Calling

Of the many unique features that the gentile relationship to the Jew holds, arguably, the most important is Israel's redemption. But there is also a shining example of a future time when the Jew will bestow upon the nations their tribal inheritance. Here it is from Ezekiel which has been referred to earlier,

> "You are to distribute this land among yourselves according to the tribes of Israel. You are to allot it as an inheritance for yourselves and for the aliens who have settled among you and who have children. You are to consider them as native-born Israelites; along with you, they are to be allotted an inheritance among the tribes of Israel. In whatever tribe the alien settles, there you are to give him his inheritance," declares the Sovereign LORD."
>
> (Ezekiel 47: 20-23.)

No other prophet speaks about the salvation and blessing of the gentiles like Isaiah. Two other prophets mention the gentiles, but only once; Jeremiah 16:19 and Malachi1:11. In Isaiah's writings, the importance of the Gentile is emphasized

15 times, and he uses the word Gentile as many times in his writings as it is used in all the rest of the OT. His prophecies are the only ones quoted in the Gospels, (Matthew 4:15–12:18–Luke 2:32.)

For sure, Isaiah is the apostle to the gentiles in the Old Testament, as the Apostle Paul is the apostle to the gentiles in the New Testament. He seems to rejoice in God's plan of salvation for all the nations. From his own words: "See, I will give a signal to the Gentiles, and they shall carry your little sons (Jewish boys) back to you in their arms, and your daughters (Jewish girls) on their shoulders" (Isaiah 49:22 the Living Bible.)

Also, the following;

> "And he said, it is a light thing that thou shouldest be my servant to raise the tribes of Jacob, and to restore the preserved of Israel: I will also give thee for a light to the Gentiles, that thou mayest be my salvation unto the end of the earth,"
>
> (Isaiah 49:6.)

As one reviews the following Scriptures, one will discover the extraordinary range of involvement that the gentile has in God's plan for the Jewish people. Honorable and profoundly prophetic, the gentiles calling are essential to God's plan for the Jewish people. Here are some examples.

- In Jeremiah 16:16, the gentiles are the gatherers of the exiled Jews and fishers of the people.
- In Isaiah 49:22, they are functioning as shepherds

guiding the Jew back to Jerusalem.
- The gentiles are seen here as philanthropists and humanitarians from Romans 15:25-27, as they share their material blessings.
- One of the areas that we first explored is the "Ruth Calling," which is a profoundly prophetic work and dramatically affecting the gentiles today.

THE CALL OF THE RUTH GENERATION

Ruth, the wife of Boaz, becomes famous for her compassion for her Jewish mother-in-law Naomi when she said these words: "Where you go I will go, and where you stay I will stay. Your people will be my people and your God my God" (Ruth 1:16 NIV.) The question that it raises; what does it mean to acknowledge a common destiny as Ruth did with Naomi?

It was nothing less than avowing a Jewish heritage. One becomes the child (adoptive or not) of a Jewish past, Jewish culture and tradition. It was the acknowledgment of oneself in a shared future with the Jew; this is a profound truth that has high relevance today. Today, countless individuals are letting go of their own gentile church culture to affirm their lot and future with the Jewish people. Often as part of the cost, it brings separation from loved ones, accusations of converting to Judaism or even erecting a wall of division.

The real benefit to the body through the Ruth generation they bring a real understanding of God's heart for His Firstborn. A modern-day Ruth's have become vital partners in the

Messianic call. Often they respond to a life's call to stand with the Jew through thick and thin. In this, their commitment stands the test of time.

GENTILES WORKING TOWARDS JEWISH RETURN: ALIYAH.

Given the persecutions and exiles of the Jewish people, the birth of Israel finally gave the Jew their homeland. Jews that return to their homeland then, fulfill what is termed, Aliyah (Return.) Aliyah resides deep in the heart of the Jewish people.

Jews living outside Israel, or the Diaspora, usually return to Israel when anti-Semitism begins, or economic difficulties arise personally or nationally. Some return due to new revelation spiritually and prophetically, and some leave to take part in their "cultural return" to live with their people in an entirely Jewish state.

Over 400 Scriptures are located in the Bible that speaks about the Jewish people returning to the land of Biblical history. The ingathering of the exiles is a timeless principle. God promised the Jewish people that they would return to the land, which began in 1948. A large portion of the Jewish people that return to Israel will do so by the assistance of the gentiles. Ministries exist today whose sole purpose is to facilitate the return of the Jewish people. Thousands of gentile believers today are serving as these shepherds' rods, pointing the Lost Sheep of Israel back to Zion.

"And kings shall be thy nursing fathers and their

queens thy nursing mothers: they shall bow down to thee with their face toward the earth, and lick up the dust of thy feet; and thou shalt know that I am the LORD: for they shall not be ashamed that wait for me,"

(Isaiah 49:2.)

"Thus saith the LORD of hosts; in those days it shall come to pass, that ten men shall take hold out of all languages of the nations, even shall take hold of the skirt of him that is a Jew, saying, we will go with you: for we have heard that God is with you,"

(Zechariah 8:23.)

SPIRITUAL ALIYAH

In addition to the geographic and cultural return of the Jewish people back to Israel, another Aliyah of sorts takes place when a gentile re-introduces a Jewish person back to their heritage after they receive Yeshua. Of course, I am speaking of a "Messianic Jewish" context. This model return bears significant results when a Jewish believer returns to their heritage, because they become a light to the greater Jewish community, and their loved ones, and friends. Dr. Daniel Juster, a well-known pioneer and writer in the Messianic movement, points out that 90% of Jewish people in America come to faith by the witness of a gentile believer.

The more significant population of Jewish people that come into Messianic congregations has come by way of gentile Christians introducing them to their heritage. It is a living practicum on the gentile role in the redemption of the Jewish people.

Also, of the many Jews that come to faith each year, many are assimilated into the gentile Christian church. But when this occurs, rarely do we witness the salvation of their loved ones as a result. Given enough time, the continuous stream of gentile church culture erodes Jewish identity to the point that the Jewish believer is no longer demonstrating a Jewish life in Messiah.

Conversely, those Jewish people that stay with their heritage, and connect with Messianic congregations, witness family salvations far more frequently; it is something that the church ignores when it comes to the Jewish harvest. It is a fact that thousands of Jewish people come to faith on any given Sunday within the Gentile Church. When one has reached their point of desperation, Jew or Gentile will bend their knee before God anywhere at any time to come into the Kingdom.

However, only in a Messianic context, can Jewish believers fill a cultural vacuum that emerges when Jewish believers enculturate into the Gentile Church to the point of forsaking their Jewish identity. It is in this process that the local Church and the Messianic Congregation can forge excellent working relationships.

PROVOKING THE JEW TO ENVY

With the gospel message falling to the gentiles after Israel's rejection of her Messiah, the gentile church has indeed proclaimed the truth of "The" One True God to virtually every nation and tongue. And for almost two, millennia's God has empowered her to testify to the power and glory of God.

As previously discussed in this book, the Gentile church was always to provoke the Jewish people to envy. It was the gentile commission to the Jew. Romans 11:11 states, "Again, I ask: Did they stumble to fall beyond recovery? Not at all! Instead, because of their transgression, salvation has come to the Gentiles to make Israel envious. Then from the same book, 10:19, "Again I ask: Did Israel not understand?

First, Moses says, "I will make you envious by those who are not a nation; I will make you angry by a nation that has no understanding." And finally, "did not the scriptures foresee that God would justify the Gentiles by faith, which was announced the in advance to Abraham, and subsequently; "all nations [ethnos] would be blessed through them" (Galatians 3:8 NIV.)

♦♦♦

What many fail to realize, Jewish culture is infamous for rehearsing history. Jewish feasts focus on historical deliverances. Other memorial days, such as Holocaust Memorial Day, and the 9th Of Av,(the darkest day in Jewish history), kept alive the sad events when both Temples were destroyed.

Starting at a young age, Jews are taught to never forget that they have suffered much at the hands of the ethnos (Nations), and yes, the New Testament church. Church leaders like the reformer Martin Luther, wrote a pamphlet in 1523, entitled; Christ Was Born a Jew. In it, he harshly criticized the Catholic

Church for presenting a pagan brand of Christianity to the Jews and expressed empathy for Jews. He said, "If I had been a Jew and had seen such fools and blockheads teach the Christian faith, I should rather have turned into a pig than become a Christian." But later Luther turned against the Jews and wrote subsequent pamphlets attacking them.

Still and all, within Christendom there has been a long-standing misunderstanding over the relationship between the Jew and the gentile—the Jew and the Christian church. Today however, the Holy Spirit is shining a new light on the stark realities of former thinking and theologies. We are evolving today with determinism to correct the wrongs of our history, and to love the Jew as our Heavenly Father intended. And as mentioned throughout this work, God is preparing the body to fulfill what may be her final mandate, the Jewish people; "The purpose of gentile salvation is to provoke the Jew to envy" (Romans 11:11.)

GENTILES STANDING AGAINST ANTI-SEMITISM

In the New Testament, the principle of God's devotion to His "First Born" is found again in the events that take place in the future Valley of Jehoshaphat. Gathered into the valley are two kinds of gentiles, goats, and sheep; the goats are the anti-Semitic nations/gentiles that have mistreated the Jewish people; the sheep/gentiles are those who supported, fed, and protected the Jewish people.

The Valley of Jehoshaphat (see also Joel 3:2,) is a naturally formed area that is shaped like a throne-seat and sits between three hills outside Jerusalem. At this location King Yeshua will gather the nations for blessing or judgment to determine who will enter through the doors of the Messianic Kingdom. The basis for the Matthew 25 judgment is again the gentile's treatment of the Jewish people (Messiah's natural brethren.) It is during this most significant time of suffering to come upon the earth, the goat gentiles due to their persecution of the Jewish people, and joining the antichrists order, forfeit their entry into the Messianic Kingdom.

This critical passage of Matthew 25:31-46, is often misquoted and used to impart a heart for missions to the poor and needy. Certainly, helping the poor and needy is central to the Gospel. But this passage deals specifically with the Jewish people and speaks of a future event that will take place upon Yeshua's return. Here is the passage,

> "when the Son of Man comes in his glory and all the angels with him, he will sit on his throne in heavenly glory. All the nations will be gathered before him, and he will separate the people one from another as a shepherd separates the sheep from the goats. He will put the sheep on his right and the goats on his left. Then the King will say to those on his right, "Come, you who are blessed by my Father; take your inheritance, the kingdom prepared for you since the creation of the world. For I was hungry, and you gave me something to eat, I was thirsty, and you gave me something to drink, I was a stranger, and you

invited me in, I needed clothes, and you clothed me, I was sick, and you looked after me, I was in prison, and you came to visit me." Then the righteous will answer him, "Lord, when did we see you hungry and feed you, or thirsty and give you something to drink? When did we see you a stranger and invite you in or needing clothes and clothe you? When did we see you sick or in prison and go to visit you?" The King will reply, "I tell you the truth, whatever you did for one of the least of these brothers of mine, you did for me." Then he will say to those on his left, "Depart from me, you who are cursed, into the eternal fire prepared for the devil and his angels. For I was hungry, and you gave me nothing to eat, I was thirsty, and you gave me nothing to drink, I was a stranger, and you did not invite me in, I needed clothes, and you did not clothe me, I was sick and in prison, and you did not look after me." They also will answer, "Lord, when did we see you hungry or thirsty or a stranger or needing clothes or sick or in prison, and did not help you?" He will reply, "I tell you the truth, whatever you did not do for one of the least of these my brethren, you did not do for me." Then they will go away to eternal punishment, but the righteous to eternal life."

(Matthew 25:31-46.)

Understanding further when the tribulation begins, all previous theories, theologies, and eschatological explanations will have proven to be correct or incorrect. In other words, one's view of

Pre-tribulation, Mid-tribulation, or Post Tribulation, will matter little since time would have proven what theology and or doctrine was correct.

In the course of this passage Yeshua's "brethren" is the source His concern; His "brethren", those according to the flesh, and natural seed of Abraham, (Matthew 10:6; John 1:11; Romans 9:5.) When the term Brethren or Brothers are used when Yeshua or Paul is speaking, they are usually addressing their Jewish brothers. So throughout the book of Acts, Paul addresses his Jewish brothers 45 times. In almost every instance he is speaking as a Jew to a Jewish audience, his brothers.

With judgment always based upon one's belief or unbelief in Yeshua, the actions of this latter group, the goat gentiles, simply expose their state of disbelief; they are persecuting the Jewish people, Messiah brethren because they have received the mark of the beast and joined the Antichrist's order. Matthew is dealing with these individuals, the goat gentiles, and as a consequence, their place in the Messianic Kingdom will be forfeited.

THE ANTICHRIST'S PLAN

Before we end this chapter, and we will review the root of a demonic agenda, and see why the end time scenario as provided by Matthew must and will take place. In the future, an unholy alliance will be made between the future anti-Christ and the goat nations, as seen in Matthew's account; satan will seek to bring a redistribution of power away from God and His people, to him and all his cohorts.

In spite of a broad move to nationalism in nations today, the end time scenario sees world governments, currencies, and financial markets merging as "foundation stones" for future world order. A periodic retreat on globalization as today does not determine prophecy. On the contrary, the Scriptures have the road set, and likely nations will return once again towards confederation for the common good.

Satan's plan though, has remained the same. As in WW II, the antichrist will likely follow the same steps as Hitler, for the corresponding author of the demonic power that consumed Hitler inspires the future anti-Christ. As Hitler consolidated his power to destroy the Jewish people, he will change international laws to gain more power and authority. Hitler enacted over four hundred specific anti-Jewish decrees based on the Nazi definition of "non-Aryan," this was to guarantee racial purity. The only difference in the anti-Christ's plan in the future is that it will be worldwide.

The anti-Messiah will forcibly enroll the world's member nations of the anti-Christ's order to fulfill his final attempt to annihilate the Jew. The Jews will again be viewed as alien to the world order as it was during WW II. And it will also be the same for born again gentile believers who refuse the mark of the beast. One can expect secret underground movements to start as they did in Europe during Hitler's reign, similar to those that my grandparents and mother began in Holland. These future underground movements will fan out across the world, drawing end-time believers to join themselves to the salvation efforts of the Jewish people.

In closing, the details of satan's end-time plan as given above, goes, of course, to a dark conspiracy to destroy the elected of God, which we have previously noted. The Prophet Isaiah in chapter 14:12-14 is the only prophet that records such exacting detail of what happened.

Listed below are satan's five "I" wills against God and the Chosen People.

♦♦♦

[1] I will a ascend into heaven. Here satan declared his desire for the highest estate that belongs to God and God alone.

[2] I will exalt myself above the stars of God. Here satan declared his desire to take over the archangel Michael's position over all the angels of heaven. Whenever the word "star "is used, it often symbolizes angels (Revelation 9:1; Amos 5:26; Judges 5:20; Psalms 147:1-5.)

[3] I will ascend above the heights of the clouds, and satan was attempting to claim the Glory, which can only belong to God. The word Cloud is associated with the glory of God; (Deuteronomy 33:26; Exodus 33:10; Exodus 34:5; Luke 21:27.)

[4] I will make myself like the Most High, he wanted to become like God and the sole possessor of the heavens and the earth and all of its inhabitants. To go higher is also to have the power to create.

[5] I will sit upon the mount of the congregation in the uttermost parts of the north, expresses his desire to rule over Israel. But satan's desires to rule are not over planets gardens or animals without souls. He was expressing his desire to rule over Israel from the uttermost parts of the North.

Also, the location of the uttermost parts of the North has always been a most valuable piece of real estate, and therefore enticing to satan; it also refers to the future throne of God in the millennial temple (Leviticus 1:11; II Kings 16:14; Ezekiel 40:46; Ezekiel 8:5; II Thessalonians 2: 4-3.)

END OF CHAPTER REFERENCES

[1] GATHERING THE EXILES: "But now I will send for many fishermen, declares the LORD, and they will catch them" (Jeremiah 16:16.)

[2] GUIDING JEWS BACK TO JERUSALEM: "This is what the Sovereign says: See, I will beckon to the Gentiles, I will lift up my banner to the peoples; they will bring your sons in their arms and carry your daughters on their shoulders" (Isaiah 49:22.)

[3] GENTILES DRAWN TO ISRAEL: "And the Gentiles shall see thy righteousness, and all kings thy glory: and thou shalt be called by a new name, which the mouth of the LORD shall name. Thou shalt also be a crown of glory in the hand of the LORD, and a royal diadem in the hand of thy God. 4 Thou shalt no more be termed Forsaken; neither shall thy land any more be termed Desolate: but thou shalt be called Hephzibah-bah, and thy land Beulah: for the LORD delighteth in thee, and thy land shall be married" (Isaiah 62:2-4.)
- Isaiah 60:3-4, "And the Gentiles shall come to thy light, and kings to the brightness of thy rising. Lift up thine eyes round about, and see: all they gather themselves together, they come to thee. The Nations will be drawn to the Glory of Israel."

[4] GENTILES RECOGNIZE GOD'S FAVOR ON THE JEW: "This is what the LORD Almighty says: "In those days ten men from all languages and nations will take firm hold of one Jew by the hem of his robe and say, "Let us go with you, because we have heard that God is with you" (Zechariah 8:23.)

[5] GENTILES PROVOKE THE JEW TO ENVY: "Again, I ask: Did they stumble to fall beyond recovery? Not at all! Rather, because of their transgression, salvation has come to the Gentiles to make Israel envious" (Romans 11:11.)

[6] GENTILES SHARE WITH THE JEWS OF THEIR MATERIAL BLESSINGS: "They were pleased to do it, and indeed they owe it to them. For if the Gentiles have shared in the Jews' spiritual blessings, they owe it to the Jews to share with them their material blessings" (Romans 15:27.)

END OF CHAPTER QUESTIONS

1. Describe the Ruth anointing from Ruth 1:16, and its implications for Jewish ministry?

2. What is Aliyah? Provide 3 Scriptural examples?

3. Explain the importance of Romans 11:11, and its work on the Christian church with regard to Jewish outreach?

4. Describe satan's fall from grace, and the 5 "I will" that forever set him against the Jewish people?

5. What prophet speaks more about the gentile than any other prophet? What is the overall message of this prophet when speaking of the gentiles?

6. What is Aliyah? Provide 3 Scriptural examples?

7. Explain the importance of Romans 11:11, and its work on the Christian church with regard to Jewish outreach?

8. Describe satan's fall from grace, and the 5 "I will" that forever set him against the Jewish people ? (Isaiah 14:12-14) ?

CHAPTER TWELVE

The One New Man

IN SCRIPTURE, A PROTOTYPE CREATION IS FOUND CALLED THE ONE NEW MAN, OR MYSTERY PLAN. Two thousand years have transpired since Rav Shaul received this understanding, and the Gentile body is seeing the One New Man in a fresh light. It has become the focal point of ministries, convocations, and conferences around the world today. Google the One New Man, and one finds a collection of ministries and theologies that span a broad spectrum of various groups and ministries.

Here we provide a summary of the One New Man to reveal what the cultural pressures were on Paul when he received this extraordinary revelation, and what many are coming to realize regarding the relationship between the Jew and gentile. One will solve a mystery as to why the One New Man relationship has never vigorously reached the physical church.

GODS MODEL PLAN

The One New Man breaks open a mystery. For Paul and those in our modern-day, an innovative and revolutionary model is found. The gentile becomes an heir with the Jew, a member together of one body, and a sharer in the greater Israel and promise in the Messiah.   In Paul's day, the One New Man had real-life application as it does today. It deregulated the rabbinic restraints that separated the Jew and gentile, and today, it tears down walls that institutional Christianity created. But go back into our ancient history when God began calling Abraham in Genesis, chapter 17, and we find the earliest prototype of the One New Man, including also some of the best touchstones to understanding the establishment of the Jewish people.

First, by brief of way introduction. Let us take in a scene for a moment that possesses all the components of an epic film. It was the time when God changed Abram's name to Abraham, and commissioned him to be the father of not only the Jewish people but most importantly, the father of the Gentiles,

> "Two rows of slaughtered animals trimmed and arranged in precise order as Abraham fights off birds of prey encircling overhead waiting to swoop down. Abraham then falls into a deep sleep, and something remarkable happens, God comes and walks amid the sacrifice to strike an unchanging pact, but not with a single man, instead, with an entire people. God changed Abram's name to Abraham that day: "Neither shall thy name any more be called Abram, but thy name shall be Abraham; for a father of many nations have I made thee."
>
> (Genesis 17:45.)

GOD'S UNORDINARY MAN

To unveil the One New Man, and we again travel back in time to Genesis 17: 4-6 to the naming ceremony of Abraham. As names were always significant in Scripture, particularly when one was given a new name, like Jacob, and whose name was changed to Israel, it was usually profoundly prophetic.

With Abraham, God fundamentally remodeled society. He affected the hearts and minds of future generations because both Jew and gentile would look back to Abraham as their spiritual father (Galatians 3:8-9; 14,16; Genesis 17:5.)

HEBREW LETTER, *HEY* ה

Reflecting on the name Abraham, God used the fifth letter of the Hebrew alphabet to form the name, Abraham. This Hebrew letter, Hey ה, provided the "h" sound in the name Abra-ham. The meaning of the letter ה Hey, is to behold or reveal. This letter seems to always provide a view into an important truth and a paradigm. Hence, we can look into Abraham to discover a treasure.

When we look into Psalms 133:1, it begins with this letter Hey. It says, "Behold, how good and how pleasant it is for brethren to dwell together in unity." What excellent benefits from unity, "it is like oil that runs down the beard of Aaron, it is as if the dew of Hermon were falling on Mount Zion, "For there the LORD bestows his blessing, even life forever."

While all Hebrew letters have numeric values, Abraham's name also increased to 248. Jewish tradition teaches that there are 248 commandments in the Torah, which comprise 248 positive actions and feelings, when these positive commandments are activated, one comes into total submission to God.

Also, the number 248 denotes unity and wholeness. 248 is a composite number, as the sum of its parts equals the whole. There are also 248 main parts of a man's body to form the whole. Therefore 248 equate to wholeness, as Abram became a whole man when his name was changed to Abraham.

Further, the letter Hey as mentioned earlier is the fifth letter of the Aleph Beis (Hebrew Alphabet.) There is a divine connection to God's grace here. Five is the number for grace. When God pours out His grace, his peace is manifest because His favor is present. Grace equates to divine favor, and it comes in many ways.

GODS NUMBER FOR GRACE

In Old Testament times there were five kinds of animals were used for sacrifices under the Old Covenant; goats, sheep, cattle, pigeons, and doves, combined they represented the way to God's grace and favor (Genesis 15:9; Exodus 29:38; Leviticus 1: 1-7; 3:1; 4:3; 14, 23; 5:6-7.) Favor and grace are shown to those that feel miserable, and it is called mercy. Favor and grace are shown to the poor, and it is called divine pity. The same is shown to the suffering, and we call it compassion. Grace and favor are also present when the body operates through the fivefold ministries that are listed in Ephesians 4:12-16.

When we turn our attention back to Abraham, Abram's

name was 243, five numbers short of God's favor. The One New Man model then points to a new reality of God's favor and grace that is awaiting us.

THE SECRET PLAN

Starting from the earlier passage in Genesis, an extraordinary event occurred when the gentile entered Abraham's lineage; the Jew and gentile were joined together for all time. In a truest sense, both the Jew and Gentile became "duty-bound" to one another when they were formed out of two parts, and made into a whole. When it comes to God's mystery plan, both cannot fulfill the model that God intended without each other.

This brings us to the meaning of "whole". From the root word Holy, "whole" and can be defined as: Not divided, in one unit, something that constitutes the full amount. The One New Man then will always bring us back to this idea of a composite creation, or, a conceptual whole. Prophetically, wholeness also equates to a sense of completeness that is coming to the Church. Of course, we are speaking of fullness and completeness that will only come by way of the Jew, not the gentile. These words are essential, "For if their rejection is the reconciliation of the world, what will their acceptance be but life from the dead" (Romans 11: 15 NIV.)

PRESERVING IDENTITY

The One New Man does "not" make gentiles into ethnic Jews. One should see both the Jew and gentile as two siblings in the same family, both , equally loved by our heavenly

Father. Both possess individual callings, yet both have unique identities. Abraham is simply and profoundly, our spiritual and prophetic forefather… a spiritual father to a natural-born heir, the Jew, and an adopted heir, the gentile.

> "After all, if you were cut out of an olive tree that is wild by nature, and contrary to nature were grafted into a cultivated olive tree, how much more readily will these, the natural branches, be grafted into their own olive tree."
>
> (Romans 11:24.)

Placed at the center of the One New Man, then, is the Scriptural teaching that Yeshua devised in Himself a unique unity apart from human regulations. Ephesians 2 and 3 reveal that it was God's intention that through the Church, that is you and I, would reveal this master plan and manifold wisdom of God. But it was also for the benefit of "rulers and authorities in the heavenly realms, "that the manifold wisdom of God might be made known through the church to the rulers and the authorities in the heavenly places" (Ephesians 3:10.)

The heavenly places spoken of in Ephesians comprise the spiritual realms, which include the three heavens in our universe (2 Corinthians 12:2.) The first heaven resides over the earth, the place of our habitation. The second is the realm of the underworld, where satan lives and where demons dwell. The third heaven is where God's throne resides.

Ephesians reveals that "all" of these spiritual realms were to witness the plan of the "One New Man." This was to be demonstrated through the material Church here on earth as stated above—the authorities in the heavenly realms. It is difficult to understand that non-human agencies were to witness the Mystery Plan along with humans. Yet, that is exactly the Father's plan. One could easily see then why it lies at the center of the historical anti-Semitism down through Christian Church history. Today, satan still seeks to separate the Jew from a gentile, especially in the midst of the many streams of new revelations today and the veil being lifted from the nations.

THE CULTURAL PRESSURES ON PAUL

Regarding the One New Man, one must grasp the enormous cultural pressure that existed in Paul's day. To begin with, Paul certainly seemed like an improbable candidate to carry the torch for the One New Man. Early on, he was the strongest opponent of the early believers. While he was a source of distrust to the believing Jews, he brought contempt and discord from the unbelieving Jews (Acts 17) upon His own completion in Messiah.

Second, I believe the One New Man invigorated Paul with new possibilities. Mainly because the Jewish people were forbidden to associate with Gentiles (Acts 10:28.) Gentiles were referred to like dogs (Mark 7:27-28.) Gentiles in the Temple area were forbidden (Acts 21:28-29) and could suffer death if they entered into the court of the Israelites. Shammai, a significant leader in Paul's day, enacted eighteen ordinances calling for a strict separation between Jews and gentiles, though his rulings were considered by some to be alienating even then.

Paul was well aware of the law of covenant proselytites, the means by which Gentiles could become partakers in the commonwealth of Israel. If gentiles submitted to circumcision, underwent mikvah (baptism,) and brought sacrifices to the temple, they could become as a native-born Israelite, and enjoy equal rights in all respects with native-born Jews'.

Proselytes (gerim,) are mentioned in Leviticus 17-25, and Philo describes the law of covenant proselytizes as a way for gentiles to become naturalized into a new and godly commonwealth. For the gentile, then, there was great enthusiasm because an easier way was before them to be welcomed into the citizenship of Israel that earlier was unattainable.

More interesting to consider, Paul never had in view the Institutional Church, Sunday Sabbath, Christian, and Catholic Holydays. There were no two conceptual frameworks of Christian living. One through Institutional Christianity, the other through the restored Jewish root we call Hebraic. Paul saw the opportunity for the Jew to finally join together as Paul saw all streams flowing in and through the One New Man. Only through this model plan called the "Mystery," could a kingdom structure and relationship be revealed.

Paul writes to the Ephesians to teach them that through Yeshua, the dividing wall between the Jew and gentile is broken down. For the first time, Paul, and those living in that day, receive an alternative program for unity outside the rabbinic—

human—regulations—A new means to scale the cultural walls that were erected between the Jew and gentile is born.

ONE NEW MAN TODAY

When it comes to our traditional understanding of the One New Man, it focuses upon a spiritual-positional truth; there is no distinction between the Jew and gentile when it comes to our standing before God and His redemptive plan. But when it comes to such glories as, sanctification, grace, and salvation, it is correct, (Galatians 3:28 and Colossians 3:11) Often however, it accompanies the idea that there is no difference in calling between the Jew and gentile. This last idea is untrue. The Jewish people have a distinct election to fulfill apart from the Gentile.

On the one hand, a similarity exists in The One New Man today from the former time. Today, the gentiles are as enthusiastic about the One New Man as they were in Paul's day. But also, the gentile is re-discovering a place in the "citizenship" of what we term this "Greater Israel." As so-called citizens in this commonwealth, speaking again of our contemporary times, the gentile enjoins themselves to the Jew and freely chooses to take part in the Biblical Feasts, Festivals, and the Biblical Sabbath (Saturday Shabbat.) They are becoming sharers in a common destiny with the Jew...similar to Ruth, who cast her lot with Naomi and said, your God shall be my God; your people shall be my people.

At the heart of this, is the gentile journeying to recapture what the church rejected—the Jewish root of New Covenant faith. Hence, the gentiles see themselves as reaching for a portion of their covenantal inheritance as co-heirs in the "Greater Israel." What they experience is nothing less than a restorative reality of the kingdom on earth.

What is this restorative reality? Jew and gentile are coming into tabernacle worship together as intended! This administration of God's kingdom, as demonstrated in the One New Man, will be restored in the Messianic Kingdom. Therefore, there is a strong prophetic element present in the migration of the gentile body to Messianic Hebraic life.

ONE NEW MAN / MESSIANIC MINISTRY

When it comes to the Messianic Jewish perspective, an end time tide has wonderfully brought in many willing gentile partners. If there is any sensitivity and concern from a Jewish perspective, it rests over the danger of diluting Jewish distinctive in Messianic Jewish life and its calling. This, of course, is a similar concern in the gentile Church when Jews lose their unique calling and identity.

The One New Man can also blur the lines between the calling of the Chosen People and the calling of the nations. This is particularly the case when gentiles begin to view themselves as ethnic Jews. And of course, there are also gentile Judaizers; people who are more captivated with Jewish elements and converting other gentiles to them.

There are also many that possess a romanticism with Israel but have little concern for the salvation of the people who make up "all Israel." Often many are apt to seize their inheritance quickly but unhurried in their desire to reach the Jew for Messiah according to Romans 11:11.

◆ ◆ ◆

Overall, this restorative Hebraic tide has become an excellent source of blessing and partnership for the end times. Messianic ministries are being used today to impart a heart for Zion and a love for Israel in these willing partners. Gentiles who come into the Messianic stream, coupled with solid kingdom teaching, spread the (Gospel of Messiah to the Jewish people efficiently and historical context that is powerful.

For sure, the believing Jews of two thousand years ago could never have imagined that the early gentiles coming to faith would be outside of the citizenship of Israel. There were no separate frameworks called Institutional Christianity, as there was no formalized Christianity as we have today with Sunday Sabbath or Christian holidays. Conversely, Paul could never have imagined either that one day believing Jews would be outside of the citizenship of the New Covenant body, mainly since it started with Jews.

As I consider the One New Man for today, a combination of several factors is driving it. First, there is a prophetic timing evident due to the closeness of the Messiah's coming. As we draw closer to all Israel coming to Messiah, the gentile body is being prepared to deal with her final mandate, all Israel. Perhaps for the first time in modern Church history, Romans 11:11 can be fulfilled in the manner in which God intended, "the purpose of gentile salvation is to provoke the Jew to envy." This will only occur if the gentile has a sincere heart for the Jew, and an understanding of their historical experiences with Christianity, otherwise they cannot provoke the Jew to envy as God intended. The One New Man then has an evangelistic quality that is paramount to God's plan for the Jew.

Second, since the Jewish foundation of Christianity collapsed early on, centuries of festal life within the gentile body was atrophying. Now the One New Man is revealing what the Institutional Church could not.

You see, by nature, institutional forms, denominations, and corporate church structures find it challenging to accept alternate streams. Everything or everyone tends to be cloned into an arrangement for comfortable management. Corporations must have this homogeneous operation. What is being stated is an unavoidable consequence of incorporating the Kingdom of God for the kingdoms of men. Praise God, Yesui will bring about a worldwide dissolution of all religious corporations.

The One New Man then possesses a Kingdom quality. Through it, God is bringing up from the deep a genetic blueprint that reveals the symbiotic relationship between the Jew and gentile, and it is finally giving to the world a picture of what the institutions should have had a long time ago. God's people are only taking back what the enemy has stolen and reclaimed their ancient rights!

◆◆◆◆

END OF CHAPTER QUESTIONS

1. Describe the "Mystery Plan" that Paul speaks of in the first three chapters of Ephesians?
2. What is the relevance of the Mystery Plan, or the One New Man today?
3. Describe the practical outworking of the One New Man when it is operating in the Christian Church?
4. What are the walls that the One New Man removes in our time? How about in Paul's time?
5. What were the cultural pressures on Paul? Provide six examples.

CONCLUSION

The words of Theodor Herzl speak to the heart of this work, "It is not the reception of the piece of literature but of an idea that makes the story." The idea's that I hope makes the story is the importance of understanding the Jewish foundation of Christianity, the evil roots of anti-Semitism, the theological right for Jews to be Israel, and the Gentile church is not the "true" and "new" Israel that has replaced the old Israel. These cannot be overstated.

In this work, we have crossed over an ecclesiastical landscape at light speed, and have built firmly upon God's Word while sifting through some of important aspects of Church and Jewish history. As the body of the Messiah has crossed over a monumental and historical threshold today, one can see portions of the body moving away from a primarily horizontal orientation; one connected to a Greek Hellenistic model that is linear-earthly; to a vertical orientation model, or a Hebraic and Kingdom model.

Consider the fact that as recently as two or three decades ago, it was not possible to speak about two different conceptual frameworks of Christian living; one Greek-Hellenic the other Hebraic-Jewish. Today, the Spirit of God has brought us to the point where such distinctions amid Church culture are being recognized and embraced. This has put out the welcome mat for Messianic Jewish ministries, Messianic Rabbis, and a host

Hebraic teaching sources that are playing an intrinsic role in this restorative work.

As a Jewish Centric Church continues to emerge, the revelation that is being brought to the body today increases the difficulty for views as "replacement theology" to survive. Though Satan will look for new hosts to counter-act it for sure, but how deep and how far this restorative work goes will be set by the readiness of the church's heart to change.

With more and more streams within Christianity awakening to the demonic roots of replacement thinking, the Christian Church is not only returning to the early days of her youth, and she is being prepared to deal with her history. Even in this, I see God making the Bride to be without spot or wrinkle upon the Messiah's return, and helping her to disentangle herself from her history. This will light the way in her finding her Last Days Mandate, "All Israel."

While the Gentile Church will self-define her role in the end-time harvest of Zion, the intercession of millions for Jewish souls and the salvation of all Israel will increase and grow stronger and stronger. The Spirit is restoring old paths of understanding and tearing down the ancient walls that have separated the Jew from a gentile.

As this wonderful work of the Spirit is progressing, we recognize the presence of the adversary too. More concise, Satan is forever initiating adversarial actions to oppose what God is doing.

- Where God gives light, Satan seeks to bring darkness.
- Where there is healing, Satan brings sickness.
- Where God gives life, Satan brings death.
- Where there is a revelation, Satan brings spiritual blindness.
- Where God is tearing down walls, Satan is erecting new walls and fortifying old walls.

You see, the enemy always seeks to subvert and to thwart where God's plans and advancements. This is the nature of the spiritual battle that has forever existed. And sadly, there is no place more central for this level and kind of warfare than in the Church. Where else should this war be waged? The Church is where this Mystery Plan was to be revealed. Therefore, we can be confident that this battle will rage stronger with every year we draw closer to Yeshua's return as well.

GOD IS ON THE MOVE

As we have unearthed passages that have been either misunderstood or obscured through the influence of anti-Semitism or sanitizing Jewish understanding from the New Testament, I invite the reader to come closer. The real voyage of discovery sees old and traditional information with new eyes.

This can mean challenging conventional wisdom, and yes, traditional theologies. This searching is a by-product of the Hebraic Renaissance of today. Caught in a dramatic shift into end-time events today, it has become a basis for some of the most dramatic transformations of Christian Church culture.

For this, I have tried to expose the practical everyday challenges that face the church in their encounter with the Jew. But historically, religious leaders in the past did not regard such questions as we have posed, to begin with. For the many topics of study that we have presented, one conclusion is certain, and catch this statement; the Jewish struggle with the Gentile Church has not always been her plain and glorious message of the Gospel, it has been her own internal rejection of all things Jewish.

Restoring the Ancient Paths is just another voice affirming an extraordinary prophetic marker for our time. In the end, will the Church ask for the ancient paths in earnest, and seek out the good way and then walk in it? (Jeremiah 6:16.)

QUESTIONS ANSWERED IN THIS STUDY

1. Can you explain the connection that the Jewish people have to Jerusalem?

2. Further, in what ways does it connect the church to the mission to reach them with the Gospel?

3. Who is founder of the State of Israel, or modern-day Zionism?

4. When did Israel become a nation, and what political organization agreed to its formation and what were the conditions?

5. Can you name Israel's three major wars, and explain what happened the day after Israel became a nation?

6. What is the ancient meaning of Jerusalem?

7. Explain the relationship of Israel to the nations from the scriptures of Isaiah 17:12 & Obadiah 1:18. In what ways does the analogy of fire and water speak to the relationship of the nations and the Jewish people?

8. What are Pogroms?

9. What are Tribunals and Crusades?

10. Describe the impact of the Holocaust in witnessing to Jewish people? What explanation can you give of an all Loving God that would allow it?

11. What did Hitler call his plan to exterminate all of European Jewry?

12. Who was Leo Frank and what Jewish organization was formed as a result?

13. Can you describe Anti-semitism? And where is it rooted?

14. What are the Protocols of the Elders of Zion? Who in American history was a primary financier of it, and helped distribute it throughout America?

15. Where did the first Jews settle, and where did they come from?

16. In 70 AD the Roman army led by Titus destroyed the Temple and sacked Jerusalem, the spiritual center of Judaism at the time.

17. In what way was the Acts 15 Jerusalem Council reflect the new Jewish leadership in this early period.

18. Following the resurrection of our Messiah they gathered on the first day of the week, which was called the Lord's Day. This evolved into the Christian Sabbath of which the Catholic Church seems to have taken claim. What is the difference between the Lord's Day, and the Sabbath which is found in the 4th commandment of the Torah. Which one should be observed?

19. Explain the foolishness of the historical charge of blaming the Jewish people for killing Jesus? What impact did it have on Judaism as well as the Church?

20. Describe the following views: Replacement Theology, Dispensationalism. Also, its impact on the mission of the Church to reach the Jew.

21. Describe Eternity and its characteristics of this future habitation.

22. Can you explain the difference between the Kingdom of God and the Kingdom of Heaven? What relevance does this have to the Jewish people and Israel?

23. Explain aspects of the Messianic Kingdom/ government upon Messiah's Second coming.

24. What is Israel's role in the Messianic Kingdom? How does this relate to the Irrevocable call in Romans 11:29 ?

25. The early church needed a new living organism or Christian expression apart from Judaism, Why? What was the impact on the Jewish people? What was the impact on the Church today?

26. In the eyes of many of His day, Yeshua was in fact the authentic Maschiach, and many accepted Him as the fulfillment of the Old Testament Prophets. Why then do the Jewish people reject Jesus as the Messiah? Give 6 reason that the leadership of Jesus day rejected.

27. The *Encyclopedia Judaica* comments about Luther's tract when it states, "Short of the Auschwitz oven and extermination, the whole Nazi Holocaust is pre-outlined here."[7] Is it any wonder that Hitler and Julius Streicher quoted Martin Luther as justification for their destruction of 6 million Jews? What impact does this have on Jewish ministry today? How do you think the

Jewish people see the Cross in comparison to a Christian? Give six reason for each.

28. The Jewish people became viewed as the rejected people of God. A people who had lost their covenantal inheritance, and the Church viewed themselves as their replacement, the new chosen people. What forms of thinking evolved that would forever erect a wall of separation between the Jewish people and the Church? Give 6 characteristics of this separation today.

29. Explain the nature of "allegorical interpretation" and the dangers it imposes upon the exegesis of God's Word? Explain 6 effects that it had on the understanding of God's heart for the Jewish people and Israel's purpose and calling.

30. Who was the founder of "allegorical interpretation," and how did he come to regarded with great respect and influence? How does the reason relate to our present times?

31. Explain the "Wife of Jehovah" passages relate to Israel, and explain the difference between the Wife of Jehovah and the Bride of Christ?

32. Explain the distinction between the Jewish people and the nations of the world? Explain the meaning of the "ethos."

33. Who was the architect of Roman Christianity that became the basis for Institutional Christianity?

34. Explain Institutional Christianity, and provide 6 characteristics?

35. Providing Acts 24:14, 25:14, how does this prove that Paul did not stop honoring the Saturday Sabbath?

36. What was the general view of the Roman world in Paul's day of the Sabbath? Explain Philo's remarks?

37. What was John the Baptists primary mission? Why was he called a forerunner (Matt 3:3; Malachi 3:1; Isaiah 40:3.)

38. What sect of Judaism is John believed to come from, and what does this say about the character of his Jewish identity?

39. What was the length of John actual ministry and explain some reasons for its short duration?

40. What is the relationship of John's ministry to the prophet Elijah? In what ways does John fulfill them and in what does it not.

41. Provide six examples of what would have happened if Israel had recognized Jesus as their long-awaited Messiah?

42. Describe the Ruth anointing from Ruth 1:16, and its implications for Jewish ministry?

43. What is Aliyah? Provide 3 Scriptural examples?

44. Explain the importance of Romans 11:11, and its work on the Christian church with regard to Jewish outreach?

45. Describe satan's fall from grace, and the 5 "I will" that forever set him against the Jewish people?

46. What prophet speaks more about the gentile than any other prophet? What is the overall message of this prophet when speaking of the gentiles?

47. What is Aliyah? Provide 3 Scriptural examples?

48. Explain the importance of Romans 11:11, and its work on the Christian church with regard to Jewish outreach?

49. Describe satan's fall from grace, and the 5 "I will" that forever set him against the Jewish people (Isaiah 14:12-14)?

50. Describe the "Mystery Plan" that Paul speaks of in the first three chapters of Ephesians?

51. What is the relevance of the Mystery Plan, or the One New Man today?

52. Describe the practical outworking of the One New Man when it is operating in the Christian Church?

53. What are the walls that the One New Man removes in our time? How about in Paul's

IMPORTANT APPENDICES TO CHAPTERS

Appendix I
(From Chapter One)

Israel's Independence
(2, 484 years to the day- 1948)
Looking back from the perspective of the present (Israel now being a nation since 1948.) Israel's War of Independence was inevitable. But her journey possesses the qualities of a great adventure story even today. The ironic truth is nations and institutions that had alienated the Jewish people from the Promised Land, unknowingly reinforced in the Jewish people an unparalleled drive to survive, and return at all costs to the Land of Biblical history. But how did the improbable become inevitable?

In Ezekiel 4:3-6, the prophet foretold that the Jews would lose control of their homeland, and would be punished for 430 years. In Ezekiel 4:3-6, God asks the prophet to act out the 430 years of punishment symbolically. Below is a brief overview of the combined prophecies of Ezekiel and Leviticus, where the actual divine formula is found when they are placed side by side. They equal and unparalleled equation of prophetic significance.

EZEKIEL PREDICTED ISRAEL'S RETURN TO THE DAY.
Bible passage: Ezekiel 4:3-6
Written: between 593-571 BC
Fulfilled: 1948
"Then take an iron pan, place it as an iron wall between you

and the city and turn your face toward it. It will be under siege, and you shall besiege it. This will be a sign to the house of Israel. "Then lie on your left side and put the sin of the house of Israel upon yourself. You are to bear their sin for the number of days you lie on your side. I have assigned you the same amount of days as the years of their sin. So, for 390 days, you will bear the sin of the house of Israel. "After you have finished this, lie down again, this time on your right side, and bear the sin of the house of Judah. I have assigned you 40 days, a day for each year."
(Ezekiel 4:3-6.)

Ezekiel records that the Jews would be punished for 430 years because they had turned away from God. As a result, the Jews lost control of their homeland, and many Jews were taken as captives to Babylon. In 539, Cyrus conquered Babylon and subsequently allowed the Jews to leave Babylon to return to their homeland. But, only a small number agreed to return, ignoring God's extended hand to end their exile. This return had taken place sometime around 536 BC, about 70 years after Judah lost independence to Babylon. Since most chose to remain in pagan Babylon, God had warned them that seven would multiply their punishment their 430 prophesied years of punishment, but minus the 70 years already served in Babylon totaled 360, i.e. (430-70= 360 years.) It is in Leviticus 26:18, 26:21, 26:24 26:28, where this perfect formula is given.

- Leviticus 26:18 - and if ye will not yet for all this hearken unto me, then I will punish you seven times more for your sins.

- Leviticus 26:21 (KJV) - And if ye walk contrary unto me, and will not hearken unto me; I will bring seven times more plagues upon you according to your sins.
- Leviticus 26:24 - Then will I also walk contrary unto you, and will punish you yet seven times for your sins.
- Leviticus 26:28 - Then I will walk contrary unto you also in a fury; and I, even I, will chastise you seven times for your sins.

By taking the remaining 360 years of punishment and multiplying by 7, you get 2,520 years. Based on Dr. Grant Jeffrey's calculations, those years are based on an ancient 360-day lunar calendar. If those years are adjusted to the modern solar calendar, the result is 2,484 years. There are precisely 2,484 years from 536 BC to 1948, which is the year that Israel regained independence.

Appendix II
(From First Law of Zion)

Review of the Covenant

There is undoubtedly no more important consequence upon the study of Israel's relationship to the Jew, and the Jew's relationship to God, than the Abrahamic Covenant. When God made a covenant with Abraham, it was the most solemn and dignified of pacts, because it was a blood covenant (the signing ceremony is recorded in Genesis 15.) Therefore, it does not provide some illusions of a relationship, and it stamps its mark of authenticity on what God established with Abraham and his heirs.

When we read about what God intended when He covenanted with Abraham, we immediately go to Genesis 17: 7-8; "I will give as an everlasting possession to you and your descendants after you, and I will be their God." But how did the land move from one to the other? Covenantal provisions never came through agreements or goodwill, or between man and man, but always between God and man. Predictably, it continuously involved a clash with other people. In 1948 when the Jewish people returned to their Land again, it came by way of opposition and violence. Israel had to settle the whole business by force when an Arab league of nations attacked them.

In ancient times in the Land of Canaan, Abraham and his

clan moved between two dominant heathenish cultures, Babylonia and Egypt. Later the patriarch Abraham was brought into the War of the Kings (Genesis 14.) It was a conflict that was comprised of an alliance of 5 kings that would ultimately sweep his nephew Lot and his household away. But Abraham is seen walking as a conqueror because God gave him a promise of an everlasting possession for him and all his generations. Similar circumstances occurred for Joshua when he had to take hold of the promise.

As the world forever struggles in formulating a definition over Israel's right to the Promised Land, the Land of Israel was given to the Jewish people not as a reward, and not as a free-will gift. It was also not independent of Israel's choices, for the blessings were dependent upon her obedience to Adonai. Compliance was always the key to the Covenantal provisions that God promised Abraham and his generations.

King Solomon found this out. The Lord became angry with Solomon because he became lofty willfully disobedient and carnally minded toward the forbidden women of other nations. The Lord said to Solomon, "Since this is your attitude and you have not kept my covenant and my decrees, I will most certainly tear the kingdom away from you and give it to one of your subordinates" (1 Kings 11:9-17). The covenantal key and its blessings were taken from Solomon, to be handed to another.

Another example is Hilkiah, the priest. Hilkiah found the lost Book of the law that had been given through Moses. He began to inquire of the Lord for himself and for the remnant in Israel and Judah about what was written in this Book. He said that the Lord's anger had been poured out on them because they had not kept the word of the Lord; they had not acted in accordance with all that was written in the Book.

But consider, no nation other than Israel can trace their claim to a historical document as the Covenant, which "The" One True God Himself inscribed. No other person as Abraham and his heirs was chosen to be custodians of its provisions. Yet obedience always unlocked the requirements of the Covenant that God made with Abraham and his heirs.

Since the covenants were either signed in blood or decreed by God's Word (the Noach and Davidic covenants were decreed,) they all shared an absolute and perpetual quality that went from one generation to the next; this speaks even for our modern day. Of course, to receive the blessings of the covenants always required obedience. From one generation to the future, the Covenant was waiting for a righteous generation to turn on its benefits.

> "Hear, O Israel, and be careful to obey so that it may go well with you and that you may increase significantly in a land flowing with milk and honey, just as the LORD, the God of your fathers, promised you".
>
> (Deuteronomy 6:3.)

COVENANT TRANSMITTED

Covenant comes from the Hebrew word berith, which we have discussed in previous chapters. This word is used throughout the Hebrew Scriptures well over two hundred times. Covenants in the Bible were a formal agreement, Jacob and Laban made a covenant with each other with specific terms to be honored in their relationship (Genesis 31:44.)

David and Jonathan struck a berith in their friendship (1 Samuel 18:3; 20:8, 16; 22:8; 23:18.) Abner struck a berith with David over his loyalty to him as king (2 Samuel 3:12-13.)

In Psalm 55:20, a berith is referred to between friends: "My companion attacks his friends; he violates his covenant." Proverbs 2:17 states, "…Who has left the partner of her youth and ignored the covenant she made before God." These covenants formed a bond between two people, between nations, between God and a single man, and between God and a specific nation, such as Israel.

As the Covenant was transmitted to Isaac then to Jacob, it provided a striking assurance of restoration to the Land with God's assurance that His promises will be fulfilled: "I am with you and will watch over you wherever you go, and I will bring you back to this Land. I will not leave you until I have done what I have promised you." Then in Genesis,

> "The LORD said to Abram after Lot had parted from him, lift up your eyes from where you are and look north and south, east and west. All the Land that you see I will give to you and your offspring forever. I will make your offspring like the dust of the earth, so that if anyone could count the dust, then your offspring could be counted. Go; walk through the length and breadth of the Land, for I am giving it to you."
> (Genesis 13:14-17.)

This is reiterated in the Davidic Covenant where God states:

> "And I will provide a place for my people Israel and will plant them so that they can have a home of their own and no longer be disturbed. Wicked people will not oppress them

anymore, as they did at the beginning and have done ever since the time I appointed leaders over my people Israel. I will also subdue all your enemies. I declare to you that the LORD will build a house for you:

(I Chronicles 17:9-10 NIV.)

THE LAND COVENANT

The second part of the land aspect of the Covenant, is wrongly referred to as the Palestinian Covenant, because it is a term coined by the Romans after the destruction of Jerusalem in AD 70, which means Philistine. Its purpose was to scorn the Jewish people with a title of their archenemies. Therefore, one will not find the word Palestine in the Bible. But the land covenant is located in Deuteronomy 30:1-10. Below is an overview:

1. Israel be scattered due to their disobedience (Deuteronomy 30:1.)
2. Israel will also repent while in their wandering (Deuteronomy 30:2.)
3. The Lord promises to return to the remnant (Deuteronomy 30:3.)
4. The Lord promises to restore the remnant (Deuteronomy 30:4-5.)
5. The Lord promises Israel national regeneration (Deuteronomy 3:6.)
6. The Lord promises Israel's enemies will be judged (Deuteronomy 30:7.)
7. The Lord promises Israel will again prosper (Deuteronomy 30:9.)
8. The Lord guarantees Israel's fulfillment (Deuteronomy

30:8-10.)

In Genesis 17:1-8 (KJV) God states;

> **And when Abram was ninety years old and nine, the LORD appeared to Abram, and said unto him, I am the Almighty God; walk before me, and be thou perfect. And I will make my Covenant between me and thee, and will multiply thee exceedingly. And Abram fell on his face: and God talked with him, saying, as for me, behold, my Covenant is with thee, and thou shalt be a father of many nations. Neither shall thy name any more be called Abram, but thy name shall be Abraham; for a father of many nations have I made thee. And I will make thee exceeding fruitful, and I will make nations of thee, and kings shall come out of thee. And I will establish my Covenant between me and thee and thy seed after thee in their generations for an everlasting covenant, to be a God unto thee, and to thy seed after thee. And I will give unto thee and to thy seed after thee, the land wherein thou art a stranger, all the Land of Canaan, for an everlasting possession; and I will be their God."**

Here God reveals specifically that the Land of Israel was not given as a short-term possession, but for the Jew's occupation forever: "All the land that you see I will give to you and your offspring forever"

The word forever, which we discussed earlier, comes from the Hebrew word ohlam. It is the same word used in many places such as Psalm 89:35-36, which states, "His seed shall endure forever, and his throne as the sun before me" (emphasis mine.) This is significant, because the nations have long downgraded this legal instrument to something no longer relevant and part of a past age and dispensation. Meditate on these words,

"Yet, in spite of this, when they are in the Land of their enemies, I will not reject them or abhor them so as to destroy them completely, breaking my Covenant with them. I am the LORD their God. But for their sake, I will remember the Covenant with their ancestors whom I brought out of Egypt in the sight of the nations to be their God. I am the LORD."

(Leviticus 26:44-45.)

Abraham's Signing Ceremony,

"So, the LORD said to him, "Bring me a heifer, a goat and a ram, each three years old, along with a dove and a young pigeon." Abram brought all these to him, cut them in two and arranged the halves opposite each other; the birds, however, he did not cut in half. Then birds of prey came down on the carcasses, but Abram drove them away. As the sun was setting, Abram fell into a deep sleep, and a thick and dreadful darkness came over him. Then the LORD said to him, "Know for certain that your descendants will be strangers in a country not their own, and they will be enslaved and mistreated four hundred years. But I will punish the nation they serve as slaves, and afterward they will come out with great possessions. You, however, will go to your fathers in peace and be buried at a good old age. In the fourth generation your descendants will come back here, for the sin of the Amorites has not yet reached its full measure." When the sun had set and darkness had fallen, a smoking firepot with a blazing torch appeared and passed between the pieces. On that day, the LORD made a covenant with Abram. He said, "To your descendants, I give this land, from the river of Egypt to the great river, the Euphrates — the land of the Knits, Kenizzites, Kadmonites, Hittites, Perizzites, Rephaites, Amorites, Canaanites, Girgashites and Jebusites."

(Genesis 15: 9-21.)

Appendix III
(From Second Law of Zion)

Letter from Gershom Salomon
2nd Law of Zion

A letter by Gershon Salomon Chairman of the Temple Mount and Land of Israel Faithful Movement Jerusalem that was delivered to President George W. Bush, he states; Cancel your anti-godly "Road Map." He passionately pleaded with President Bush, and I quote from the excerpt; "President Bush, please obey the Word of the G-d of Israel and the universe as it appears above. Immediately cancel your anti-godly "Road Map" and your plans to divide the Land of Israel and to establish an evil, anti-godly so-called "Palestinian" state in the midst of the Land of the G-d and the people of Israel. When Mr. Olmert comes to you please reject him and his anti-godly plans and tell him to return immediately to Jerusalem and to ask permission not from you but from the real Leader of all the world who dwells in Jerusalem, the Almighty G-d of Abraham, Isaac and Jacob. Surely He will reject such an evil and anti-godly plan. He will teach him His Real Road Map through the Covenant that He made with the people and the Land of Israel ". He states further; President Bush, you represent a nation that loves Israel. Please do not accept or support these anti-godly plans of Prime Minister Olmert and don't bring the American nation and yourself under the judgment of G-d which is soon to come not only on an Israeli Prime Minister who created and wishes to fulfill such an evil plan but maybe especially on you if you support and encourage such a plan. The United States of America was created more than 200 years ago not to be against the G-d and the people of Israel but to stand with and support Israel in her struggle to reestablish the Kingdom of the G-d and the people of Israel in the holy Land of Israel. It is the G-d of Israel Himself that pushed down your popularity among your own people after you created another plan to divide the Land of Israel by the so-called "Road Map". There is only one Road Map. This is the Road Map, which G-d gave to Abraham and to his seed Israel more than 4,000 years ago when He sent him to the Land of Israel, the Land that you (President Bush) want to divide now together with Prime Minister Olmert. Please read the Word of G-d, and it will save you from a mistake

Appendix IV
(From Fourth Law of Zion)

Jewish Achievements
Medicine

- Dr. Abraham Waksman coined the term antibiotics.
- Dr. Paul "magic bullet" Ehrlich won the Nobel Prize in 1908 for curing syphilis.
- Dr. Abraham Jacobi is known as America's father pediatrics.
- Dr. Simon Baruch performed the first successful operation for appendicitis.
- Casmir Funk, a Polish Jew, pioneered a new field of medical research and coined the word vitamins.

Business and Finance

- Haym Solomon and Isaac Moses created the first modern-banking institution. Jews created the first department stores: Altman's, Gimbels, Kaufmanns, Lazarus's, Magnins, Mays, and Strauss's all became leaders of major department stores. Julius Rosendale revolutionized the way Americans purchased goods by improving Sears Roebuck's mail-order merchandising.
- Hart, Schaffner, Marx, Kuppenheimer, and Levi Strauss became household names in men's clothing.
- Isadore and Nathan Straus - "Abraham & Strauss"

became the sole owners of Macy's, the world's largest department store.
- Armand Hammer (Arm & Hammer) was a physician and businessman who originated the most significant trade between the U.S. And Russia.
- Louis Santanel was the financier who provided the funds for Columbus' voyage to America.

Entertainment

- Samuel Goldwyn and Louis B. Mayer (MGM) produced the first full-length sound picture, The Jazz Singer.
- European Jews are the founding fathers of all the Hollywood studios.
- Adolph Zukor built the first theater used to show motion pictures.
- George and Ira Gershwin and Irving Berlin are three of the most prolific composers of the twentieth century.
- Sherry Lansing of Paramount became the first woman president of a major Hollywood studio.
- Steven Spielberg is the most successful filmmaker since the advent of film.

Famous Jewish Actors & Musicians

Henry Winkler (the Fonzie) / Charlie Chaplin / Clark Gable / Woody Allen / Jeff Bridges / James Brolin / Mel Brooks / George Burns / Ben Stiller / Harrison Ford / Art Garfunkel / Carly Simon / Phil Silvers /William Shatner/ Peter Sellers / Jerry Seinfeld / Adam Sandler / Edward G. Robinson /

Don Rickles / Leonard Nimoy / Marilyn Monroe / Zero Mostel / Bette Midler / Walter Matthau /Jackie Mason / Marx Brothers / Barry Manilow /Jerry Lewis/ Richard Dreyfus / Billy Crystal / Bob Dylan / Barbra Streisand/Soupy Sales / The Three Stooges / Lauren Bacall / Jack Benny.

Inventions

- Theodor Judah was chief architect and engineer of the first American transcontinental railroad.

- In 1909, four Jews were among the sixty multicultural signers of the call to the National Action, which resulted in the creation of the NAACO.

- In 1910 Louis Balustein and his son opened the first gas station, eventually founding Amoco Oil. In 1918 Max Goldberg opened the first commercial parking lot, located in Detroit.

- Emile Berliner developed the modern-day phonograph. The machine he patented was called the gramophone. Berliner made possible the modern record industry. The Victor Talking Machine Company, now known as RCA, absorbed his company.
  The first printing press was invented by a Jewish person in **1563 in Asia**

Telecommunications

- A Jewish person in the Israeli branch of Motorola developed the cell phone.

- Jewish people developed most of the Windows NT and

XP operating systems.

- A Jewish person at Intel Corporation designed the Pentium MMX chip technology.
- The Pentium 4 microprocessor and the Centrino processor were developed, designed, and produced by Jewish people in Israel.

Exploration and Art

- A Jewish person concluded before all others that the world was round (Judah Cresaques, better known as "Map Jew".)
- The first man to set foot in the New World was not Columbus but his Jewish interpreter, Rodrigo Sanches.
- Jewish financier Haymin Salomon supported the American Revolution.
- Jewish composer Irving Berlin composed the song "God Bless America."
- Jewish artist Marc Chagall's stained glass "peace window" adorns a wall in the United Nations building.
- Jewish poet Emma Lazarus wrote the inscription on the Statue of Liberty: "Give me your tired···your poor··· your huddled masses.

Economics

- Israel, the 100th smallest country, with 1/1000th of the world's population, has a $100 billion economy that is larger than all of its immediate neighbors' combined.
- Israel has the highest ratio of university degrees and

produces more scientific papers per capita than any other nation.

- Israel has the highest average living standards in the Middle East.

- Twenty-four percent of Israel's workforce holds university degrees, ranking third in the industrialized world, after the United States and the Netherlands.

- Israel is the only country that entered the twenty-first century with a net gain in its number of trees, a remarkable achievement considering the desert land that it is.

Foods and Ice Cream

- Ben & Jerry's were founded in 1977 by Ben Cohen and Jerry Greenfield with $12,000.

- Tom Carvel, of Greek Jewish descent, who arrived in New York in 1910, founded Carvel Ice Cream.

- David Mintz, born in Williamsburg, created Tofutti, the world-famous dairy-free ice cream, Brooklyn.

- Hebrew National was founded by Isadore Pinckowitz, a Romanian immigrant butcher who began his career peddling meat from the back of a horse-drawn wagon. Pinckowitz (later known as Isadore Pines) bought the Hebrew National Kosher Sausage Factory in 1928.

- Ruben and Rose Mattus, Polish Jews, founded Haagen-Dazs.

Spiritually and Prophetically

- God chose the Jewish people to be head of the nation's Deuteronomy 28:13, 44.)
- God chose the Jewish people to transmit the Word of God to future generations (Romans 3:1-2.)
- God chose the Jewish people for an end-time worldwide revival (Revelation 7:1-14.)
- The Jewish people hold the key to the second coming (Matthew 23:39; Hosea 5:15.)
- The Jewish people will determine who enters the Messianic Kingdom by the nation's treatment of them during Jacob's Trouble, or the Great Tribulation, (Matthew 25).
- The Jewish people will also confer upon the Gentile the tribe of their choosing in the age to come, (Ezekiel 47:23).
- The Jewish people were chosen to bring the Messiah to the World, and first in the infilling of the Holy Spirit (Acts 1-2.)

ENDNOTES

Authors Note: 1 Susan Stroomenbergh Halpern, *Memoirs of the War Years – The Netherlands 1940-1945, A Christian Perspective* [First Edition, Copyright 2002) Vantage Press, Inc. New York, NY 10001.

Introduction: Restorative Streams

1. Emil Schurer, D.D., M.A., *A History of the Jewish People* (Third Edition – April 1998, Volume 1, First Division.
2. *Time Magazine, March 24, 2008 (Cover* Story: 10 Ideas that are changing the world.) Page 60 #10, *"Re-Judaizing Jesus"*
3. Cliff Hanger: Something that leaves one in a precarious or difficult dilemma. In literature it leaves the audience with a hope to see how the characters resolve the dilemma. With Israel, the world will one day see how they resolve this dilemma with the final return of Messiah.
4. *Kairos* is a Greek word that, in the New Testament, refers to an appointed time in God's purpose.

Chapter 1: Visionary for Zion

1. Jack Friedman, *The Jerusalem Book of Quotations: A 3,000 – Year Perspective. Gefen Publishing House, Lynbrook, NY 11563
2. *Special Life Magazine Edition/Israel's Swift Victory* © 1967.
3. The Other Case for Defensible Borders/Richard Bell 1978 *carta*, Jerusalem, The Revolt / by Menachem Begin/ Nash Publishing, Los Angeles 1948.
4. Rabbi Hayim Halevy Donin, *To Be a Jew*/ Basic Books, Inc.

Publishers, *New York 1972.*

5. William Whiston, A.M., *The Works of Josephus*/ Book IV P 546 *(Fourteenth Edition)* March 1999 Hendrickson Publishers, Inc, Peabody, Massachusetts.

6. Praeger, Edited by Alvin Z. Rubinstein, *The Arab-Israeli Conflict*; Praeger Publishers, New York 1984.

7. *The Time,* London, May 5, 1938.

Chapter 2: Fire and Water: Understanding Historical Anti-Semitism.

1. The Hebrew English Edition of the Babylonian Talmud; *Tractate Berakoth*

2. Martin Gilbert, *The Atlas of Jewish History*/William Morrow and Company, Inc. New York. 1969

3. 2. Abram Leon Sachar, *A History of the Jews (Fifth Edition)* (New York: Alfred A. Knopf, 1967,) 251.

4. Dennis Prager and Joseph Telushkin, *Why the Jews: The Reason for Anti-Semitism*/ A Touch Stone Book, Simon & Schuster, Inc. 1983

5. *Der Stürmer* (literally, "The Stormer;" or more accurately, "The Attacker") was a weekly Nazi newspaper published by Julius Streicher from 1923 to the end of World War II in 1945, with brief suspensions in publication due to legal difficulties. It was a significant part of the Nazi propaganda machinery and was vehemently anti-Semitic / http://en.wikipedia.org/wiki/Der Sturmer.

6. The Story of the Jew`/ Rabbi Lee J. Levinger/ Behrman House, Inc. New York.

7. Dennis Prager and Joseph Telushkin, *Why the Jews: The Reason for Anti-Semitism/ A Touch Stone Book, Simon & Schuster, Inc. 1983*

8. David A. Altshuler / Hilter's War Against the Jews/ Behrman House, Inc. New York 1978.

Chapter 3: Into the Melting Pot: Anti-Semitism in America.

1. Arthur Hertzberg. The Jews in America; four centuries of an uneasy encounter, Simon and Schuster 1989. P 24

2. Dennis Prager and Joseph Telushkin. *Why The Jews: The Reason for Anti-Semitism.* Touchstone Book, Published by Simon & Shuster, Inc, New York 1983.

3. Rosie G. Lurie. *American Jewish Heroes*. The Union of American Hebrew Congregations, 1968.

4. Ibid

5. Arthur Hertzberg. The Jews in America; four centuries of an uneasy encounter, Simon and Schuster 1989.

6. Seth S. Wenger, *The Jewish Americans: Three Centuries of Jewish Voices in America.* Doubleday Publishers 2007.

7. Louis Harap. *The Image of the Jew in American Literature,* The Jewish Publication Society, 1974.

8. Ibid

9. http://www.usconstitution.net/jeffwall.html/
http://nobeliefs.com/jefferson.htm

10. Ibid.

11. Gordon W. Allport, *The Nature of Prejudice*: 25th Anniversary Edition Gordon W. Allport, Kenneth Clark, Thomas Pettigrew: Books. 1979.

Chapter 4: Law of Zion

1. Rabbi Hayim Halevy Donin. *To Be a Jew,* Basic Books, Inc. Publications, New York. 1972.

1st Law of Zion/The Law of the Covenant.

1. Self-Evidence: The principle of self-evidence applies even to salvation; "For since the creation of the world God's invisible qualities, his eternal power and divine nature have been clearly seen, being understood from what has been made, so that men are without excuse." Romans 1:20 (NIV) In other words, a world that is the handiwork of God establishes a scale of self-evidence that a divine Creator is involved.

2. "Inalienable Rights" was defined as "Rights which are not capable of being surrendered or transferred without the consent of the one possessing such rights" (According to *Morrison v. State*, Mo. App., 252 S.W.2d 97, 101..) Unalienable rights are those that are "incapable of being alienated, that is, sold and transferred." It meant under no circumstances could one's rights be given to another.

3. English Common Law / to understand more of the nature of ancient law, we go back to early understanding of *English Common Law* with respect to land ownership. In times past, land could only be inherited; it could not be given away, sold, or granted to another person. Which brings us back to Genesis 13:14: *"All the land that you see I will give to you and your offspring forever."* Hence, it could only move from one generation to the next.

2nd Law of Zion:

1. William Koenig. *Eye to Eye: Facing the consequences of Dividing* Israel, About Him Publishing, Alexandria, VA 22313 20062.

The listings below are given merely to help the reader explore further. The author takes no responsibility for extraneous material oftentimes posted on sites by others.

 American Foreign *Policy-Israel* and *Natural Disasters*...Jan 10, 2010... Since 1990, every time the American government has tried to fiddle with the borders of *Israel*, some kind of *natural disaster* has occurred **to...***God'ssecret.wordpress.com/.../american-foreign-policy-israel-and-natural-disasters.*

Correlations between Foreign *Policy* Relating to *Israel* and *Natural*...2 posts - 1 author discussion about Correlations between Foreign *Policy* Relating to *Israel* and *Natural Disasters* in the AboveTopSecret.com website alternative topics discussion...
www.abovetopsecret.com/forum/thread534602/pg1

American Foreign *Policy-Israel* and *Natural Disasters* Discussion about American Foreign *Policy-Israel* and *Natural Disasters* at the Godlike Productions Conspiracy Forum. Our topics include Conspiracy Theory,
www.godlikeproductions.com/forum1/message961947/pg1

1. America's anti *Israel* stance linked to *natural disasters*!

McTernan" links the timing of economic disasters and *natural disasters* to... President Obama's foreign *policy* regarding *Israel* is literally a recipe for...*www.sodahead.com/...anti-Israel...natural-disasters/blog-158617/*

2. Tough menu to swallow - Haaretz - *Israel* News Jul 12, 2009... The restrictive *Israeli policy* only encourages the opening of unofficial... or malnutrition brought on as a result of a *natural disaster....www.haaretz.com/hasen/spages/1099179.html*

3. Israel War, Hurricanes, Earthquakes & Natural Disasters - Breaking...Find *Israel* breaking news on war, hurricanes, earthquakes & *natural disasters* at **all voices**, where anyone can report from anywhere. **All voices** is the only... **www.allvoices.com/Israel/disasters**.

www.thedailygreen/environment-news/latest/2007-weather extremes Bernard Reich/ *The United States and Israel*. Praeger Publishers 198 CBS Educational and Professional Publishing. New York.

3rd Law of Zion:
1. http://bostonreview.net/BR34.3/malhotra_margalit.php

4th Law of Zion. *References taken from the following:*
1. *Start –Up-Nation/ The Story of Israel's Economic Miracle, Dan* Senor and Saul Singer, 12 Twelve Publishing, New York,

237 Park Avenue New York, NY 10017, 2009.

2. *Senor and Saul Singer / a Council on Foreign Relations Book.*

3. Arthur Hertzberg, *The Jews In America*/Simon and Shuster.1989 by Arthur Hertzberg- Louis Harap, *The Image of The Jew In American Literature,* The Jewish Publication Society of America.1974.

4. Darryl Lymann, *Great Jews In Entertainment*, Jonathan David Publishers, Inc., Middle Village, New York, 11379. 2005.

5. Dan Cohn-Sherbok, *Dictionary of JEWISH Biography*, Oxford University Press 2005Ernest.

6. Beth Wenger, *The Jewish Americans,* Double Day, New York, 2007.

7. Van Den Haag, *The Jewish Mystique.* Stein and Day Publishers, New York 1969

Chapter 5: Unlocking Israel's Election

1. (*Eric Hoffer, Reflections, "Washington Daily News, May 28,1968.)*
2. The Epistle to Barnabas, translation in Holmes ed. *The Apostolic Fathers, 270-327.*
3. Israel and the Church / Jacques B. Doukan, p55
4. John Pawlikowski, Jesus and the Theology of Israel (Wilmington, Del, Michael Glazier, 1989.)
5. Israel And The Church / Jacques B. Doukan / Dan Cohn-Sherbok, The Cruciified Jew: Twenty Centuries of Christian

Anti-Semitism (Grand Rapids; Eerdmans, 1997 (31-320.)

Chapter 6: Israel & The Messianic Kingdom

Isaiah 65.20 "No longer will there be an infant *who lives but a few* days, or an old man who does not live out his days; For the youth will die at the age of one hundred And the one who does not reach the age of one hundred will be *thought* accursed." All those who do not reach the age of 100 years will have died due to some sin that has brought pre-mature death; every person will have the chance to live at least to 1000.

Deuteronomy 32.8 *"When the Most High gave the nations their inheritance, when he divided all mankind, he set up boundaries for the peoples according to the number of the sons of Israel."* Here one can presume that when Messiah returns, as he will finally settle Israel securely into their land, but also will settle the nations within their God given boundaries. (Acts 17:26.)

1. Tractate Sanhedrin, London, the Soncino Press 1994 (Hebrew-English Edition of the Babylonian Talmud.) Sanhedrin was the council of state and supreme tribunal of the Jewish people during the century of or more preceding the fall of the Second Temple. It consisted of seventy-one members, and was presided by over by the High Priest.

Chapter 7: The Feasts of The Lord

1. Sabbath: Its Meaning For Modern Man / Abraham Heschel

/ Samson Raphael Hirsche, Farrar, Srauss, and Giroux/ 10 Union Square West, New York 10003 / copyright 1951 Abraham Heschel.

2. Samuel Raphael Hirsch / June 20 1808 – December 31 1888) was a German rabbi best known as the intellectual founder of the Torah" Derech Eretz school of contemporary Orthodox Judaism, he occasionally termed *neo-Orthodoxy*, his philosophy, together with that of Azriel Hildesheimer, has had a considerable influence on the development of Orthodox Judaism.[1] Hirsch was rabbi in Oldenburg, Emden, was subsequently appointed chief rabbi of Moravia, and from 1851 until his death led the secessionist Orthodox community in Frankfurt am Main. He wrote a number of influential books, and for a number of years published the monthly journal Jeschurun, in which he outlined his philosophy of Judaism.

3. Occasions where Christ spoke during the Feasts:
Passover (Matt. 26: 1-2, 17-29; Mark 14:12-26;
Luke 22:7-38; John 2:13-25; 11:55-56; 13:1-30; 1 Cor. 5:7)
Tabernacles (John 7:2-37)
Sabbath (Matt. 12:1-14; Mark 2:23-35; Luke 4:16-30; 6:1-10; 13:10-16; 14: 1-5; John 5:1-15; 9:1-34; Acts 13:14-48)
Yom Kippur (Acts 27:9; Rom. 3:24-26; Heb. 9:1-14; 23-26)
Feast of Dedication" (John 10:22-39)
    Festival of Weeks — Pentecost (Acts 2:1-41; 20:16; 1 Cor. 15:16:8)
    Unleavened Bread (Matt. 26:17; Mark 14:1,12; Luke 22: 1,7;

Acts 12:3; 20:6; 1 Cor. 5:6)

4. **Pesachim 54a** of the Talmud, deals with the name of the Messiah, and seven things were created before the world was created.

5. Rabbi Gerald J. Catano, Reflections on Belove Prayers and Favorite Essays from the Hebrew Liturgy.

6. 1. David (1 Kings 11:33,) 2. Asa (1 Kings 15:11,) 3. Jehoshaphat" (1 Kings 22:43,) 4. Jehoash (2 Kings 12:2,) 5. Amaziah (2 Kings 14:3,) 6. Uzziah (2 Kings 15:3,) 7. Jotham (2 Kings 15:34,) 8. Hezekiah (2 Kings 18:3,) 9. Josiah (2 Kings 22:2.)

7. Jacques B. Doukhan, *Israel And The Church: The Voices for the same God. Hendrickson Publishers*, Peabody Massachusetts 01961-3473. Copywrite 2002 by Hendrickson.

8. Christianity the Empire Religion: Christianity began as a religion of the state of Rome. It was politically and economically convenient to join. It was under a single supreme authority, Emperor Constantine; it developed into a large commercial organization even then. It was the first shadow on earth of the One World Order-One World Religion.

Chapter 8: The Jewish Root Severed

1. Rabban Yochanan ben Zakkai is credited with saving the Torah and Judaism itself upon the Roman Armies assault upon Jerusalem in 70 A.D Torah. This great spiritual leader at

the time conceived a plan to make believe he was dead. Soon a small processional marched his believed dead body out of the besieged Jerusalem, and as soon as he was clear from the city, he went to" the Romans General's tent to plea for safe passage to Yavneh.

2. John Pawlikowski, *Jesus and the Theology of Israel*, Wilmington, Delaware. Michael Glazier, 1989, 10-11

3. The speech in Defense of Lucius Flaccus, *Cicero* (Loeb Classical Library,) volume.10, 441.

4. David H. Stern, *Restoring The Jewishness Of the Gospel. Jewish New Testament P* in 306 AD was an ecclesiastical synod held in Elvira in what was then the Roman province of Hispania Baetica, which ranks among the more important provincial synods, for the breadth of its canons. Its date cannot be determined with exactness, but is believed to be in the first quarter of the fourth century, approximately 305-306. It was one of three councils, together with the Synod of Arles and the Synod of Ancyra that first approached the character of general councils and prepared the way for the first ecumenical council: Information taken from http://en.wikipedia.org/wiki/Synod_of_Elvira.

6. Bruce R. Booker. *The Lie; Exposing the Satanic Plot Behind Anti-Semitism.* Brentwood Academic Press, Columbus Georgia, 1993.

Richard Booker. *How the Cross Became a Sword,* Sounds of the Trumpet, Inc. 4747 Research Forest Drive, The Woodlands,

TX 77381, 1994

7. Encyclopedia Judaica on line: *Publications, Inc. Clarksville, Md. Copy write 1988.* Synod of Elvira http://www.jewishencyclopedia.com/view.jsp?artid=631&letter=L&search=Luther.

8. Dr. Michael Brown, *Our Hands Are Stained With Blood.* Destiny Image Publishers, Inc. Shippensburg, Pa 1992

Chapter 9: A Theological Thievery

1. Dan Gruber, *The Church and the Jews: The Biblical Relationship. Elijah Publishing, P.O. Box 3595, Hanover, NH 03755, Copy write 1997*

2. Philip Schaff, *History of the Christian Church, Volume 2.* Hendrickson Publishers, Peabody Massachusetts, 1996

3. ABRAHAM JOSHUA HESCHEL. *THE ALLEGORIZATION OF THE BIBLE, PDF* http://www.bunyanministries.org/books/israel_and_millennialism/23_app_m_allegorization%20of%20the%20Bible.pdf

4. Jack Jacobs and Ed Rogers, *Becoming One.* Echod Publishing, New City, NY. 2006. P60

5. ABRAHAM JOSHUA HESCHEL. *THE ALLEGORIZATION OF THE BIBLE, PDF* http://www.bunyanministries.org/books/israel_and_millennialism/23_app_m_allegorization%20of%20the%20Bible.pdf

6. Jacques B. Doukhan. *Israel And The Church* Hendrickson Publishers, Peabody Massachusetts, 2002, p 78-79,96.

Chapter 10: Sabbath and Torah

1. William Whiston, A.M., *The Works of Josephus*. Hendrickson Publishers, Peabody Massachusetts, Inc. 1987.

2. Philo, The Special Laws, II/ p 574, Complete and Unabridged – New Updated Version.

3. Emil Shurer, D.D., M.A., *Life Under the Law: A History of the Jewish People in the Time of Jesus Christ, Volume II / Hendrickson Publishers, Peabody Massachusetts 1890, 1998.*

4. Richard Booker, No Longer Strangers.

5. Edward Synan, *The Popes And The Jews In The Middle Ages*, The Macmillan 6. ompany, New York, NY, Copy write, Edward A. Synan 1965.

6. *Ethics of the Fathers*, Avoth, Chapter 1 (Judaica Press.)

Yosef Yitzhak Lifshitz, *Secret of the Sabbath/* Winter 5761 / 2001, no. 10. http://www.azure.org.il/article.php?id=280

Chapter 11: Misconception/Restorations (John The Baptist and Elijah)

1. Judah Macabee: The Jewish feast of Hanukkah ("Dedication") commemorates the restoration of Jewish worship at the temple in Jerusalem in 165 BCE, after Judah Maccabee removed the pagan statuary.

2. Tractate Eduyyoth 9b

3. Ruling over nations: See Luke 19; Revelation 5:10; 2 Timothy 2:12

4. Nation of Israel: We continually refer to national Israel because it was religious leadership that rejected Messiah's Messianic claims. Hundreds of thousands of Jews did accept Him. But Messiah came to restore the nation of Israel first.

Chapter 11: The Gentiles Find Their Calling

1. Mutually beneficial relationship: a cooperative, mutually beneficial relationship between two people or groups (*Encarta ® World English Dictionary* © 1998-2004 Microsoft Corporation. All rights reserved.)

2. Revelation 7:4-8: "Then I heard the number of those who were sealed: 144,000 from all the tribes of Israel. From the tribe of Judah 12,000 were sealed, from the tribe of Reuben 12,000, from the tribe of Gad 12,000, from the tribe of Asher 12,000, from the tribe of Naphtali 12,000, from the tribe of Manasseh 12,000, from the tribe of Simeon 12,000, from the tribe of Levi 12,000, from the tribe of Issachar 12,000, from the tribe of Zebulun 12,000, from the tribe of Joseph 12,000, from the tribe of Benjamin 12,000."

1. Revelation 7:9-15: "After this I looked and there before me was a great multitude that no one could count, from every nation, tribe, people and language, standing before the throne and in front of the Lamb. They were wearing white robes and were holding palm branches in their hands. And they cried out in a loud voice: 'Salvation belongs to our God, who sits on the throne, and to the Lamb.' All the angels were standing around the throne and around the elders and the four living creatures. They fell down on their faces before the throne and worshiped God, saying: 'Amen! Praise and glory and wisdom and thanks and honor and power and strength are to our God forever and ever. Amen!'

- **Isaiah 11:10** "In that day the Root of Jesse will stand as a banner for the peoples; the nations will rally to him, and his place of rest will be glorious."

- **Isaiah 25:6** "On this mountain the LORD Almighty will prepare a feast of rich food for all peoples, a banquet of aged wine—the best of meats and the finest of wines."

- **Isaiah 25:7** "On this mountain he will destroy the shroud that enfolds all peoples, the sheet that covers all nations.

- **Isaiah 42:1** "Here is my servant, whom I uphold, my chosen one in whom I delight; I will put my Spirit on him and he will bring justice to the nations."

- **Isaiah 61:9** "And their seed shall be known among the Gentiles, and their offspring among the people: all that see them shall acknowledge them, that they are the seed which the LORD hath blessed."

Isaiah 60:3-4 "And the Gentiles shall come to thy light, and kings to the brightness of thy rising. Lift up thine eyes round about, and see: all they gather themselves together, they come to thee."   *** The gentiles will be drawn to the glory of Israel:**

- **Isaiah 62:2-4:** "And the Gentiles shall see thy righteousness, and all kings thy glory: and thou shalt be called by a new name, which the mouth of the LORD shall name. Thou shalt also be a crown of glory in the hand of the LORD, and a royal diadem in the hand of thy God. Thou shalt no more be termed Forsaken; neither shall thy land any more be termed Desolate: but thou shalt be called Hephzi-bah, and thy land Beulah: for the LORD delighteth in thee and thy land shall be married."

- **Zechariah 8:23:** "This is what the LORD Almighty states: 'In those days ten men from all languages and nations will take firm hold of one Jew by the hem of his robe and say, "Let us go with you, because we have heard that God is with you."

Chapter 13 The One New Man

George Foot Moore, *Judaism, Volume I"* Hendrickson Publishe

BIBLIOGRAPHY

Bridger, David, ed., and Wolk, Rabbi Samuel. *The New Jewish Encyclopedia*. J.S.D / Behrman House Inc. 1976.

Cohn-Sherbock, Dan. *Dictionary of Jewish Biography*. Oxford University Press 2005.

Donin, Rabbi Hayim Halevy. *To Be a Jew*. Basic Books Inc. Publishers 2001.

Flint, Peter W. *The Bible at Qumran: Text, Shape, and Interpretation*. Wm. B. Eerdmans Publishing Co. 2001.

Foley, Michael P. *Wedding Rites: A Complete Guide to Traditional Vows, Music, Ceremonies, Blessings and Interfaith Services*. Wm. B. Eerdmans Publishing Co. 2008.

Gersh, Harry. *When a Jew Celebrates*. Behrman House Inc. 1971.

Gilbert, Martin. *The Atlas of Jewish History*. William Morrow & Co. Inc. 1995.

Harap, Louis. *The Image of the Jew in American Literature*. Syracuse University Press 2003.

Hertzberg, Arthur. *The Jews in America*. Simon & Schuster 1998.

Hull, William L. *The Fall and Rise of Israel*. Zondervan Publishing House 1954.

Krohn, Paysach J. *Bris Milah: Circumcision – The Covenant of*

Abraham. Mesorah Publications Ltd. 1985.

Losh, Richard R. *All the People in the Bible: An A-Z Guide to the Saints, Scoundrels, and Other Characters in Scripture*. Wm. B. Eerdmans Publishing Co. 2008.

Lymann, Darryl. *Great Jews in Entertainment*. Jonathan David Publications Inc. 2005.

Margolis, Morris B. *Twenty Twenty: Jewish Visionaries Through Two Thousand Years*. Jason Aronson Inc. 2000.

Mendes, Paul R., and Reinharz, Jehuda. *The Jew in the Modern World: A Documentary History*. Oxford University Press 1980.

Newman, Louis E. *An Introduction to Jewish Ethics*. Pearson Education Inc. 2005.

Prager, Dennis, and Telushkin, Joseph. *Why the Jews? The Reason for Anti-Semitism*. Simon & Schuster 1983

Samuels, Ruth. *Pathways Through Jewish History*. Ktav Publishing House Inc. 1967.

Scheinbaum, A.L. *Peninim on the Torah: An Anthology of Thought Provoking Ideas and Practical Insights on the Weekly Parsha*. Peninim Publications 2005.

Senor, Dan, and Singer, Saul. *Start-Up Nation: The Story of Israel's Economic Miracle*. Twelve 2009.

Stroomenbergh Halpern, Susan. *Memoirs of the War Years 2008: The Netherlands, 1940-1945*

A Christian Perspective. Vantage Press Inc.

Tcherikover, Victor. *Hellenistic Civilization and the Jews.* Hendrickson Publishers Inc. 1999.

Unterman, Alan. *Dictionary of Jewish Lore & Legend.* Thames and Hudson Inc. 1997.

VandenHaag, Ernest. *The Jewish Mystique.* Stein and Day Publishers 1969.

Wegner, Beth S. *The Jewish Americans.* Doubleday 2007.

4.The Saperstein Edition/ Rashi/ Bereishis-Genesis, p. 114.

GLOSSARY

Adonai: Hebrew name of God meaning "my Lord."

Adonai Elohenu: The Lord our God.

Adon olam: Eternal Lord.

Amidah Prayer: The standing prayer known as shemoneh esreh or the "eighteen benedictions."

Antinomianism: The belief that faith frees a person from all obligations to observe the law of God. It can also be seen in an attitude of hostility towards God's law.

Benei Yisrael : Children of Israel.

Chofesh: Freedom, liberty

Commonwealth: A people who are united by a common interest such as a state or nation (Israel.) Today, gentiles are once becoming part of this commonwealth of Israel.

Diaspora: The Greek word meaning dispersion has been applied to all Jewish people and communities outside of Israel.

Eliyahu ha-Navi: Elijah the prophet.

Elohim: God

El Shaddai: God Most High

Erets Yisrael: Land of Israel.

Ha-Shem: The Name (of God.)

Ivri: Means Hebrew.

Ivrim: The Hebrews.

Mitzvah: The Hebrew word of commandment or good deed.

Moed: Appointment, A fixed time or season.

Moedim: Plural for Moed, and speaks of all the Feasts (Appointed Times..)

Ru'ach: Wind, air, breath, soul, spirit.

Ru'ach chayim: Breath of life.

Ru'ach Adonai: Breath of God.

Ruach HaKodesh: Holy spirit.

Shabbat: The Hebrew word for Sabbath.

Siddur: The Jewish prayer book.

Shema: Shema Yisrael (or Sh'ma Yisrael; Hebrew: שְׁמַע יִשְׂרָאֵל; "Hear, [O] Israel") are the first two words of a section of the Torah, and is the title (sometimes shortened to simply **Shema**) of a prayer that serves as a centerpiece of the morning and evening Jewish prayer services

Tanakh: The Hebrew term for the entire Old Testament, and is comprised of the three sections; the Torah (first section in the bible comprised of the Five books of Moses,) Nevi'im, the Hebrew prophets, and the Ketuvim, the Writings.

Teshuva. Repentance, return.

Torah: The Hebrew term for the first five books of the Old Testament known as the Five Books of Moses.

Yisrael: He, who strives with God, may God rule.

Yeshua: Yeshua is the original Hebrew proper name for Jesus of Nazareth. In Hebrew Yeshua means both "Salvation" and the form of Yahoshua, the "L-RD who is Salvation

ABOUT THE AUTHOR

Felix Halpern was born in 1952 in the Netherlands. As a child his family immigrated to the United States, where he was raised in the Northern New Jersey area. Prior to full-time ministry, he established a lucrative career in the precious metals and diamond industries located in the International Diamond Center of New York City. There immersed for nearly two decades in the Orthodox and Hassidic Jewish communities, he understands well the heart of the Jewish people.

Coming from a rich Jewish heritage himself, it is one that is also rooted in Nazi resistance. Rabbi Halpern's paternal Grandfather was an Orthodox rabbi and leader of his own synagogue in Germany, and his maternal Grandparents established one of the many underground resistance movements against Hitler throughout the Netherlands. It is also where his Father received the knowledge and understanding of his Messiah while being hidden with other Jews, after miraculously escaping Germany.

Throughout a large portion of his life, Rabbi Halpern lived outside of Judaism. But later due to God's sovereign intervention, he was brought back to his heritage to carry out his destiny to the "Lost Sheep of the House of Israel." From this experience, he distinguishes himself as a "Moses Jew," or, Jews who have lived for large portions of their lives unaware of their Judaism. Like Moses who lived most of his life as an Egyptian and unaware of his Judaism until later in life, Felix reclaimed his birthright as a "Moses Generation" Jew. He notes;

"I myself had little knowledge for most of my life that my destiny to the Lost Sheep of the House of Israel would be rooted in this seed of Jewish identity, one that remained dormant for half my life. It was then through a sovereign encounter of the spiritual suffering of our people that thrust myself and family into a full-time call. Characteristic of many Jewish believers in Messiah, he was influenced by the notion that Jews are no longer Jewish when they come to faith. Felix began to understand this unscriptural theology and its anti-Semitic roots, and began to petition the Lord to restore his Jewish understanding of the Scriptures coupled with a specific request to restore the rabbinic eyes of his Orthodox Jewish grandfather.

Following three months of earnest prayer, the Lord miraculously responded with a dynamic restoration of new vision, and new understanding of the Scriptures. Particularly, those passages relating to Israel, the church and the last days. Further, breaking down the walls that Replacement Theology erects in fully understanding Scripture.

In obedience to the Lord's call and restoration, Felix immediately resigned his position as Vice President of Sales and Marketing for a multimillion-dollar international company, liquidated his family's savings and retirement monies, and embarked upon a life of faith and complete dependency on the Lord's provision. With over a decade of God's sufficiency and provision, their lives testify to the wonderful faithfulness of God, as well as the Lord's restoration of his Jewish heritage that characterizes his life and family today.

Ministry Today

Today, Felix Halpern ministers internationally with a message of restoration between Jew and Gentile, and a strong burden to bring the Father's Love to the nations. Ministering on restoring the Jewish roots of New Covenant faith, and a strong emphasis on the election of Israel, Felix fulfills this role to the Church with a zeal and fervor of the end times.

Over the last decade, he was instrumental in forming the first National Jewish Fellowship of the Assemblies of God, and has served the first four years as its President. He has also served as a General Presbyter for the Assemblies of God, on the AG Board of Ethnicity, and also on the board of Lost Lamb Evangelistic Association. In 2013 God provide the means to form the first Resource Office for Jewish Ministry within the Assemblies of God in the Greater New York, and New Jersey Metropolitan region.

Felix Halpern serves as a nationally appointed missionary to the Jewish people, and for twenty years he and his wife Bonnie served as Senior leaders of a Messianic Congregation that they founded, Beth Chofesh, (House of Freedom.

Bonnie Halpern

Bonnie Halpern his wife was born in 1956 in Brooklyn, and is a fellow pioneer. Serving together, they are a unique couple, both Jewish, that brings not only solid marital success and wisdom to couples and families, but Bonnie ministers with anointing to empower women in these end times.

Growing up in a traditional Jewish home, Bonnie throughout her adolescent years searched for God and had many supernatural encounters with her Messiah. Her journey to faith is the basis of a powerful testimony today, as she ministers in and out of the body, sharing her testimony to Jew and gentile alike. A dedicated and successful mother of two young women, Bonnie also coaches women in the areas of household disciplines, finances, organizational skills, as well as parenting and nutrition.

Bonnie is a highly gifted speaker that brings to the body of Messiah a firm calling to release women into a Deborah anointing. She also ministers and teaches as a Nutritional Consultant, educating and training the body on the "Keys to Physical and Spiritual Health." Bonnie continually demonstrates her passion for maintaining the physical health of the body, as well as teaching on practical and easy methods for helping believers maintain their "temples."

Felix and Bonnie Halpern have been happily married for over forty years, and have raised two daughters and reside in the New Jersey area.

FILMS AND BOOKS OF AUTHORS DESCENDANTS

The USC Shoah Foundation Institute for Visual History and Education, established by Steven Spielberg, taped a story for the United States Holocaust Memorial Museum library that included the testimony of his father and Rabbi Halpern's grandfather, an Orthodox Jewish rabbi of a synagogue in Germany. Spielberg's film shares his father's story—one of survival as an Orthodox Jewish boy escaping Nazi-occupied Germany who found himself in the hands of the Dutch underground to save him. The film is a poignant picture that testifies to the millions of Jews whose lives were forever altered, generations that were blighted from history.

Rabbi Halpern's maternal side claims a heritage of resistance against the Nazis. The story is chronicled in a book authored by his mother, Susan Stroomenbergh-Halpern, titled *Memoirs of the War Years: The Netherlands, 1940–1945: A Christian Perspective*. It is the story of a Dutch family's valiant efforts to launch a resistance movement against the Nazis on behalf of the Jewish people.

The family's efforts were recognized on December 22, 1997, at the Righteous Among the Nations Ceremony held at the Israeli Embassy in New York by Consul General Colette Avital. Rabbi Halpern's mother and maternal grandparents received medals and documents to memorialize their sacrifices.

TO CONTACT RABBI FELIX
AND BONNIE HALPERN

WRITE:

Metro Jewish Resources
P.O. BOX 3777
WAYNE, N J
07474-3777

www.metrojewishag.org /
email: metrojrag@gmail.com

www.ingramcontent.com/pod-product-compliance
Lightning Source LLC
Chambersburg PA
CBHW031410290426
44110CB00011B/325